make it yours with mimi g

Editors: Meredith A. Clark, Shawna Mullen
Designer: Jenice Kim
Managing Editor: Glenn Ramirez
Production Manager: Rachael Marks

Library of Congress Control Number: 2022944491

ISBN: 978-1-4197-5948-2
eISBN: 979-8-88707-057-5

Text copyright © 2023 Mimi G. Ford
Photographs by Norris Danta Ford
Illustrations by Josée Perreault, JP Fashion Studio

Cover © 2023 Abrams

Printed and bound in China
10 9 8 7 6 5 4 3 2 1

Abrams books are available at special discounts when purchased in quantity
for premiums and promotions as well as fundraising or educational use.
Special editions can also be created to specification. For details, contact
specialsales@abramsbooks.com or the address below.

Abrams® is a registered trademark of Harry N. Abrams, Inc.

ABRAMS The Art of Books
195 Broadway, New York, NY 10007
abramsbooks.com

make it yours with mimi g

A Sewist's Guide to a Custom Wardrobe

Mimi G. Ford

ABRAMS, NEW YORK

contents

introduction

When I decided to start Mimi G Style Inc. in 2012, my purpose was to share my love of sewing. I didn't imagine that my blog would become so popular or that just a year after founding Mimi G Style I would quit my day job in film and production to become the first blogger licensee for Simplicity Patterns. I loved making videos and taking pictures of the things I was making for myself, and I realized that I might be able to turn my hobby into a business, so that's what I did. I focused on teaching and showing people that #sewingissexy, the first hashtag I started back in 2008. Sewing for me was very normal; I grew up visiting my family in Puerto Rico every summer and most of my time there was spent in my aunt's studio watching her turn fabric into beautiful wedding and formal gowns. I was fascinated by the idea of turning a piece of fabric into something wearable, so like I assume many of us did, I started sewing for my Barbie.

Not long after I started showing interest, my father bought me my first sewing machine, and I became obsessed! I started taking apart my clothes, tracing them onto new fabric, and sewing them up. I didn't know it at the time, but I was teaching myself construction. I sewed on and off as a kid until I experienced homeless in my late teens. I didn't pick it back up until I was in my late twenties, but it was as if I had never stopped—my love of sewing was reignited. I haven't stopped sewing since, but I never imagined my hobby would become what it is today. I remember the first several comments from fans and followers: "You make sewing sexy." I hadn't thought of it that way, but it was true. I had seen a ton of quilting, kids sewing, and home décor blogs, but there weren't many people who focused on fashion sewing. I wanted everyone to see how fun and sexy sewing could be, and beyond the actual sewing, my blog had a lot to do with fashion and personal style. I have always been a fashion junkie, and this was my way of making things I loved that were designed for my curvy Latina body. My excitement for sewing, fashion, and teaching catapulted my blog, and I haven't stopped pushing forward since.

When I signed my first licensing deal with Simplicity, I was so worried people wouldn't like the patterns. I remember going over and over my designs, making sure they were perfect and true to my style. Eight years later my patterns are still bestsellers, and I am now the vice president of design for Simplicity, McCall's, Butterick, Vogue Patterns, and New Look. I sometimes can't believe this is my life. I launched Sew It Academy in 2016 with the hopes of creating an educational platform for sewing and design, and to date we have more than fifty thousand enrolled students. I am fortunate to work with major brands on product development. I cofounded a fabric store and creative center in Atlanta, Georgia, and recently launched a new academy for pattern making.

When I started blogging years ago, I never imagined that someday I would write my own book. I also never imagined that I would have my own line of patterns, or that I would be featured in *Forbes* magazine, or that I would build a multimillion-dollar business from teaching others to sew, or that I would create a community of hundreds of thousands of sewing-obsessed fans who I love so very much. Yet, with all the success I have been blessed with, the one thing that gives me the most joy is teaching and watching my students grow into amazing and talented makers. When you are a runaway teen from Chicago who ends up on the streets of Los Angeles at fifteen years old, you never quite imagine that you can build a life of purpose and service, so when I look back on my life, I do so with a smile, because it has taught me all that I know. I am grateful for all the good, bad, and even terrible moments that have led me to this time in my life, writing this book—for you. I am a proud mom of four amazing kids who continuously keep me laughing and spend countless hours teaching me how to properly use TikTok. My husband is my right-hand man who works with me on all the crazy ideas I have and has never once hesitated. He is my rock, and there is no way I could manage all of this without him. I believe that everything in life truly is possible, and I am a testament to that. I hope you enjoy creating a wardrobe that you can customize to fit your lifestyle and wear year-round.

how to use this book

I spent a lot of time deciding what I wanted you to get out of this book because I believe that patterns are simply a guide, a place for you to start, and that you should allow for your own creativity, personal style, and fit preference to come to life. I didn't want this book to be solely about DIY, I wanted it to be about fashion sewing! I have taught tens of thousands of students to sew over the years, and the one thing many of them had in common was their hesitancy to modify the pattern and make it theirs. That is why I want to give you the power to create and make the garments you love without fear or limitations. This book is a guide to creating a wardrobe you can be proud of, that will speak to who you are and help you sew up garments that make you feel your best. I coined a phrase many years ago—"Sewing Is Sexy"—and that is how you should feel when you make and wear your clothes. You should be confident, comfortable, empowered by your skill, and sexy, in whatever form that means to you.

This book contains seven base patterns. The designs are what I would consider to be my favorite shapes. These seven patterns will be transformed into eighteen total patterns with simple pattern hacks to give you a year-round wardrobe that you'll design based on your choice of fit, length, fabrics, trims, and style.

Further along in the book I will share some tips on choosing fabrics, mixing prints, and really expanding your thinking when it comes to making a pattern your own. You will see how I take these eighteen patterns and create a wardrobe with more than one hundred looks that you can be inspired by. But first there are some basics I need to cover, like getting your space set up with the tools and equipment you will need. Let's get started!

what you will learn

I am excited to join you on this journey of creating pieces you really love. In doing so, you will learn how simple modifications to a pattern can give you completely different looks, how fabric choice can make the same pattern look completely different, and how fun and easy it is to slash and spread a pattern to turn a shirt into a jacket, or a button-up into a dress, or pleated trousers into wide-leg pants, or a t-shirt into a dress. The possibilities are endless! I thought of forty more modifications for each base pattern as I was working them out, and so will you as you start to hack away and expand your imagination.

tools and supplies

It's always easier to start a project knowing exactly what you need to complete it. I approach sewing much like I approach cooking: I start with a clean workspace, gather everything I am going to need, and then I start. Having the right tools will eliminate a lot of frustration and will make sewing a lot more fun. Sometimes the issue you may be having when working on a project is that you don't have the right tool for the job. These basic sewing tools are always in my studio and have made my life so much easier. Some you will recognize, and some you may have seen and wondered if you "really" needed them; trust me, you do!

THREAD

For most sewing projects an *all-purpose polyester thread* will do. There are a few other options to consider based on your fabric choice, but a high-quality all-purpose poly thread is ideal for most fabrics due to its strength and elasticity. That doesn't mean the thread is stretchy like an elastic thread you would use for shirring, but it has "give," whereas a *cotton thread* has no give at all and is used most often in quilting. *Silk thread* is used on very delicate fabrics, mainly to hand baste or in tailoring due to its strength and invisibility when you meld it into the fabric during pressing. *Topstitching thread* is thicker and often used for decorative stitching.

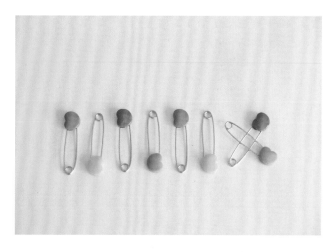

PINS

You would be amazed at how many types of pins there are; they come with flat heads, plastic heads, glass heads, and metal. Pins also come in different shaft lengths and widths and with different points. I am just going to cover the most common dressmaking pins.

1. *Glass head pins* are great for pinning thick layers, as they are strong and won't melt.
2. *Silk pins* come in a variety of sizes, including fine and extra fine, and are great for pinning delicate fabrics without leaving a large piercing.
3. *Ball point pins* are great for pinning knit fabrics; much like your sewing machine needle, it won't break the fabric thread.

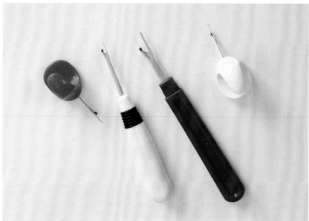

SEAM RIPPER (AKA YOUR BESTIE)

The seam ripper is most likely your best friend when you need it, but it's also your nemesis, because if you are using it, you probably made a mistake and need to unpick your stitches.

CUTTING TOOLS

I am going to start by saying you should never, ever, ever use the same scissors for cutting paper and fabric. The fastest way to dull your dressmaking shears is to also cut your paper patterns with them. Trust me when I say that you should have a pair for cutting patterns and paper in general and a great pair of *dressmaking shears* that you only use to cut fabric. Let's be honest, cutting is probably the part of sewing most of us dislike most. You can, however, make your life easier by using a good-quality pair with sharp blades, or in my case, I use a *rotary cutter*! Many years ago, I started getting pain in my wrist, so I turned in my scissors for a rotary

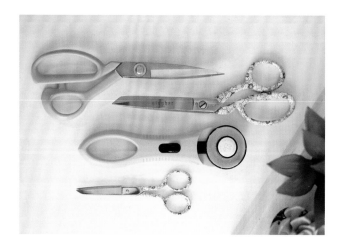

cutter and never looked back. It is so much faster to cut with and very precise, but you do need a *self-healing cutting mat*. Now when I pick up scissors, they seem foreign to me, and I simply can't cut as neatly as I can with my rotary cutter. *Thread nippers* are also a great tool to have near your sewing machine. I use them to clean up loose threads as I work.

MEASURING TOOLS

You need a *soft tape measure* for taking your body measurements and checking measurements as you sew. I also recommend you have a *yard stick* and a *clear 2" x 18" (5 x 45.7 cm) plastic ruler*.

French curve and *hip curve rulers* are great for drawing curves. They can often be found for a reasonable price, and I suggest you have them in your sewing space. They are very handy, and we will be using them in this book.

MARKING TOOLS

- **Marking Pens and Chalk:** You will use a variety of marking tools over time; it all depends on your fabric. You should have *markers* that disappear with water or air, *tailors chalk* or *chalk rollers*, and *marking pencils* that come in a variety of colors. My favorite tool is the Dritz Mark-B-Gone pen.
- **Seam Gauge:** I can't live without my seam gauge! It makes marking hems, seam allowances, waistbands, and button placements fast and easy.

PRESSING TOOLS

Pressing is the most important thing you can do while sewing. Seams that have not been properly pressed are the first telltale sign of a "home sewn" garment. When you sew a seam, you press a seam, so it is best that you have the right tools. Aside from a great *iron* and *ironing table* or surface, here are some useful tools I always make sure to have.

A *tailor's ham* is used to help you press and mold darts, curved seams, sleeve caps, and collars.

The *seam roll* is great for getting into sleeves and to prevent seam allowances and hems from creating an impression on the right side of your fabric when you iron. I use it often to press my seams open.

Pressing cloths are used as a barrier between your fabric and the iron sole plate. I lay my pressing cloth on my fabric and then place my iron on my fabric to avoid any scorching or shine marks. I always purchase a yard of silk organza and cut it into twelve-inch squares. This one yard will generally last me a very long time.

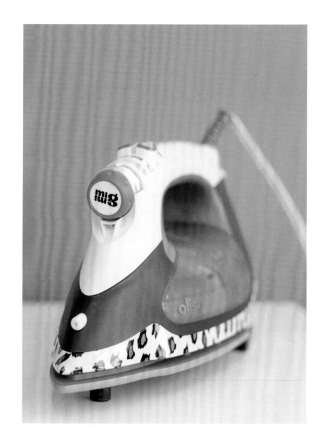

DRAFTING TOOLS

You will be tracing patterns and hacking patterns in this book, so you will need the following supplies in your space.

1. *Pattern tracing paper* is a must. You will use this to trace your patterns, but you will also use it for our hacks. I order a big roll of dotted pattern paper (see Resources, page 176), but you can also use any large roll of paper, like old gift-wrapping paper, medical paper rolls, or even craft paper rolls.

2. Pens, pencils, markers, and coloring pencils: You will be using a graphite pencil during the hacking process, but colored pencils are useful to mark style lines and fit adjustments. I use a Sharpie marker to accurately label my patterns.

3. A *needle-point tracing wheel* is a great tool for transferring darts, grainlines, and pattern changes onto your new paper. This tracing wheel has sharp needle-like points that create small markings or perforations on your paper that you can see and feel.

4. A *pattern notcher* is not a must-have tool, but I certainly use it often. It makes a small cutout wherever you need a notch on your pattern. As we modify our patterns to create new styles, a notcher will come in handy.

PATTERN WEIGHTS

There are a ton of pattern weights you can buy, but I usually just buy a bunch of large washers from my local home improvement store; they work like a charm and are cheap.

MUSLIN

Muslin is an inexpensive cotton fabric that is used to make a test garment of the pattern you are working with to work out any fit issues before cutting into your fashion fabric. You can purchase muslin by the yard or roll, but you can also use old sheets you may have at home. I encourage you to make a muslin of all the base patterns in this book. This will allow you to make any fit adjustments to the base pattern before we start to hack and create other styles.

POINT AND LOOP TURNERS

I own a variety of point and loop turners. They are great for pushing out corners and pressing creases. Loop turners are helpful for turning thin straps and come in variety of sizes.

THE SEWING MACHINE

It goes without saying that you need a sewing machine. All you really need is a machine that produces a good straight stitch, a zigzag stitch, and a buttonhole. The fancy stitches and bells and whistles are cool, but even with a top-of-the-line, fully loaded sewing machine like the one I have, I only use a straight stitch and a narrow zigzag 90 percent of the time. I always purchase my sewing machine based on how well it makes a buttonhole—it is non-negotiable for me.

5. *Manila paper* is also something I keep on hand. When I draft a pattern, I transfer it to manila paper because it's strong and will not tear or crumple like regular paper.

6. *Pattern hooks* are what I use to hang my patterns. I really don't like folding them or rolling them up, and since they are usually made from manila paper it makes it easier to store and see what the pattern is. You can buy these online for just a few bucks.

7. *Tape*—lots of it! When modifying and slashing and spreading your base patterns, you will need tape, so make sure to stock up.

THE SERGER

A serger is great machine to have in your sewing room if your budget allows for it. It sews the seam, trims your fabric, and finishes the raw edge simultaneously. It is wonderful for sewing knit fabrics and giving you a professional-looking finish on your seams, as it prevents knit seam allowances from rolling. When working with fabrics that tend to fray, encasing the raw edge with a serged overlock stitch prevents your fabric from fraying further in the wash, but you can also prevent this with a zigzag stitch on your sewing machine if you don't have a serger.

PRESSER FEET

For this book you will be using your *basic presser foot* along with a *zipper foot* and a *buttonhole foot*. These usually come with your machine, so there is no need to purchase them. Another handy presser foot I love is the *edgestitch foot*. I use it often for stitching in the ditch and sewing along the edges of pockets and waistbands, for example. I also truly love my *walking foot*, which I use when sewing with knits and slippery fabrics.

SEWING MACHINE NEEDLES

Having a variety of needles on hand will make sewing much easier. Although universal needles can be used for many fabrics, there are fabrics that need specific needles: knits, denim, leather, and silk. I keep *jersey or ball point needles* in my studio for knits; the medium ballpoint helps to slip between the knit fibers and won't break or damage them while sewing.

Denim needles are strong and sharp, which helps you to sew through multiple layers without your needle breaking. *Leather needles* are very sharp with the eye closer to the tip of the needle, which helps to puncture through the leather. I use *microtex needles* for sewing silks and satins. Microtex needles are extra-thin and pierce the fabric quickly to avoid snagging; they were developed for sewing modern microfibers and other finely woven fabrics, so they're great for sewing easily damaged fabrics. I also love *topstitching needles* for when I am working on denim and having beautiful topstitching is a must.

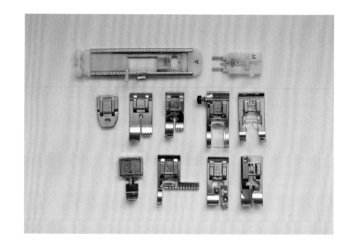

let's talk fabric

This topic alone can be a book, because there is so much I could cover, but let's keep it simple. Fabric choice can make or break your garment, and over my years of teaching I've seen it is an area many students struggle with. Knowing the technical names of fabrics—much like you see on the back of commercial pattern envelopes—can help, and I give some recommended fabric choices for each base pattern. But you should feel free to explore different fabrics.

Let's say you want to make an A-line skirt. If you were to use a rayon, the "hand" of the rayon—the way it will feel against your body—is going to be soft and will drape nicely against your body. If you make the same skirt from a denim or a twill, you will have a more structured A-line skirt that will sit away from the body. Neither fabric is right or wrong because it is a style preference. Obviously, there are fabrics that won't work as

well for a garment based on weight, thickness, or hand, but deciding on these factors is very much a personal choice. The only "rule" you should always consider is that if the garment was designed for a knit you should use a knit fabric, and if it was designed for a woven use a woven fabric. In the past, I have made a pattern that was designed for a woven out of a knit, but this requires some experience and knowledge; if you don't feel comfortable, stick with the rule.

Shopping for fabric can be tricky, especially when you are doing so online, so I tell my students to get familiar with the fabric content in their ready-to-wear garments so they can identify similar content blends in the description of fabrics they are buying. It's also a really good idea to make a swatch book as you purchase fabrics: write down the name and content of your fabric on an index card and staple a small square of the fabric to it. Before you know it, you will start to understand fabric content and how it behaves, and shopping online won't be such a mystery.

my go-to woven fabrics

I strongly believe in choosing quality fabrics for your me-made garments, because if you are spending time making something from scratch and adding your personal touches to it, you want it to last! However, if you are new to sewing or just starting out, then by all means use inexpensive fabrics, old sheets, or thrifted finds until you feel confident enough in your skill to use a good piece of fashion fabric. There are designs in this book for woven fabrics and for knits, so let's talk about some of my favorite fabrics to work with.

COTTON

Cotton is a very common fiber; it is relatively affordable and can be found as a blend in many garments. You may be familiar with 100 percent quilting cotton, which is sometimes stiffer than cotton blends. You can always find cotton fabric in a ton of solids and prints, and it is a great fabric for everyday wear. Cotton and cotton blends are nice for button-up shirts, shirtdresses, pants, dresses, and skirts.

SHIRTING

Shirting fabric is a broad term that refers to a tightly woven fabric and tends to be less sheer than other cottons.

TWILL

Twill is very versatile; it is a type of cotton weave. The weave is characterized by diagonal lines. This is done by passing the weft thread over one or more warp threads and then under two or more warp threads. Medium-weight twill is great for pants, jackets, and blazers. Lightweight twill is great for shirts and dresses.

LINEN

What is not to love about linen? It is used a lot for summer makes because it is lightweight and has great breathability. Linen, much like cotton, can be found in blends. One of my favorite blends is a linen/rayon. This blend has a soft hand and a more fluid drape than 100 percent linen, which makes it perfect for dresses and tops. Linen also comes in various weights and finishes, like "washed linen," which gives you a soft, worn look and feel. Linen comes in many solid colors, woven stripes, and checks, and sometimes you can find a great linen print.

DENIM

Denim comes in so many weights, colors, and finishes, and of course with and without stretch (in the form of spandex) woven in. I love sewing with denim and have made many denim garments over the years. From jackets and skirts to jeans, dresses, and accessories, denim is always a great choice for many of your projects.

TIPS: There are a few things about working with denim you should know.

- As you start sewing and joining seams, your layers will get thick, so try your best to trim your seam allowances when you can.
- Always use a special denim needle; this will help your machine sew through thick layers without breaking your needle.
- Topstitching is key when sewing denim garments, so use a topstitching thread—but never use it in your bobbin. Just fill your bobbin with all-purpose thread of the same color.
- Always prewash your denim to prevent your garment from shrinking after you've sewn it. Prewashing will also get rid of the excess blue dye that can sometimes stain your hands and your machine.

CORDUROY

Corduroy is a strong durable fabric with a rounded rib, or wale, surface. The back usually has a plain or twill weave. The width of the cord is referred to as the size of the wale, which is the number of ridges per inch. The lower the wale, the thicker the cord width. This is a great fabric for outerwear, pants, and structured skirts. You can also find corduroy with stretch, which makes wearing finished garments much more comfortable.

CREPE

This is one of my favorite fabrics to work with. Crepe is a silk, wool, rayon, or synthetic fabric with a noticeably wrinkled or bumpy look, with some natural mechanical stretch due to the tightly twisted yarns.

- *Crepe de Chine* is very common in garment sewing. It is lightweight and mainly made from silk but doesn't have the same wrinkled or bumpy texture common to other crepes. Polyester crepe de chine is readily available and is more affordable, and it looks just as great.

RAYON

Fabrics made from rayon are a good option for so many garments. The result of the chemical process that creates rayon threads is a soft but strong fabric that is lightweight and durable. Rayon can be woven into many types of fabric, like twill, crepe, or sateen. You can find many types of rayon in solids and prints. They are perfect for tops, flowing skirts, pants, and dresses.

The really great thing about rayon is how many options you have when it comes to the source of the fiber. Bamboo rayon is at the top of my list. My other favorite is rayon challis, a very lightweight fabric that can be slippery to work with. I will often cut my pieces one at a time as opposed to cutting two with the fabric folded onto itself, as I believe it makes for a more accurate cut.

my go-to knit fabrics

I think knit fabrics get a bad rap, as they can be scary for new sewists to work with—but if you know the basics of working with knits, they can be a lot of fun. The first thing you need to know is to use the correct needle. I always suggest testing a scrap of the knit fabric you plan to use with different needles until you get the right look. I can generally sew most knits with a ball point needle or stretch needle but sometimes if the knit fabric is delicate, I have found that a microtex needle works well. The use of a walking foot can help the knit layers feed evenly through your feed dogs.

COTTON SPANDEX

This is a common, easy to find knit. It comes in a range of weights and thicknesses and has a 4-way stretch. It's a great choice for many garments, especially t-shirts, skirts, and leggings, and the heavier weights work well in the fall and winter months when you may want to make a turtleneck or long-sleeve knit tops. It has great stretch and recovery!

COTTON JERSEY

This knit is on the lighter side and can be found in both two-way and four-way stretch. Two-way fabric stretches two ways, crosswise, and a four-way fabric stretches in all four ways, crosswise and lengthwise. It can be a bit fussy to work with and can curl at the cut edge, but pinning can help with that. I find that spraying the cut edge with starch and pressing it will help keep the cut edge flat.

LIVERPOOL KNIT

I love Liverpool knit and I carry a lot of it in my fabric store. It is on the heavier side and has a bumpy texture like you might find on a crepe. It has great stretch and is very opaque. It works well for pants, tops, dresses, and cardigans.

SWEATER KNITS

Sweater knit is a great fabric for the warmer months. It is a go-to for my cardigans and pullovers because it is soft and warm. You can find sweater knits in a variety of weights, in cabled or plain knit, and in various colors and prints.

RIBBED KNITS

This is a very specific knit that has ribbing running through it. It is perfect for tanks, neckbands, cuffs, and waistbands, but it can also be used for full garments like fitted and semi-fitted dresses.

DOUBLE KNITS

I have to say that I have become known for using double knits (also called "ponte knits") over the years. I love the weight of a great double knit (DK) and it comes with various amounts of stretch. The best thing about a DK is that you can use it as a woven, it holds up great, and it keeps its shape.

Interfacings

Interfacing is a stabilizer. It is used to give firmness, crispness, and stability to collars, cuffs, waistbands, and facings. It is not seen, as it is usually sandwiched between fabric layers. You have two options when it comes to interfacing: fusible and sew-in. As you can probably guess, the fusible has a heat-activated adhesive on one side; it is easy to work with and once ironed on will become a permanent part of your fabric. It works well with most fabrics other than those that do not do well with heat, like leather or nylon. Sew-in interfacings are often used in couture garments and are a good option to use on fabrics that have a lot of texture or can't be ironed.

Interfacings are tricky because they will change the hand and drape of your fabric. You can easily add too much weight or stiffness to your fabric, so it's always best to test a swatch first. I have two types of interfacing in my studio: woven and knit.

WOVEN INTERFACINGS

You can find woven interfacings in breathable and natural fibers, and they are perfect for many different garments. Woven interfacing looks and feels very much like a regular woven fabric and has a selvedge edge, so you want to make sure to cut following the grainline.

You also have the option of using fashion fabrics such as muslin, batiste, and silk organza as interfacing.

KNIT INTERFACINGS

Knit interfacings are softer and have more drape than a woven interfacing, and they allow for stretch. Knit interfacings are great for facings and waistbands on knit garments.

nap and directional prints

Directional prints are a type of fabric design where the design faces or goes in one direction only. If you turn the fabric around, you will notice that the design is upside down or facing another direction. Usually, you want directional prints to all face the same way in your garment—you don't want the print to face up on the front of a dress but be upside down on the back. When using a directional print, make sure that when you lay your pattern pieces on the fabric you are placing them in the correct direction.

Nap follows the same rule as directional prints: The pattern pieces must be cut going the correct direction on the fabric. Two great examples of nap are velvet and corduroy: both have raised surfaces called pile. You can cut napped fabrics with the nap running either down or up the garment (described as "with the nap" or "against the nap"). Rubbing down the length of the pile is going with the nap; rubbing up the length is going against the nap. The fibers lie smooth and flat with the nap and feel slightly rough against the nap. Colors also can look darker or lighter based on the direction the nap runs in a garment.

pretreating your fabric

Before cutting into your fashion fabric, you should pretreat it the same way you plan to treat the finished garment. If you plan to wash and dry it, then wash and dry your fabric yardage. If you plan to have the garment dry cleaned only, then there is no need to pretreat it, but make sure you dry clean it after completing the sewing. The reason for prewashing your fabrics is to prevent the garment shrinking after you have sewn it. You want the shrinkage to happen in the wash before you cut out your pattern pieces. This will keep you from crying because you didn't pretreat and it shrunk after you spent time sewing it—trust me, I speak from experience. Pretreating also removes fabric sizing and finishers some people may be sensitive to, as well as dust from shipping and display in a store.

choosing a needle

Needle choice is not rocket science—you can generally find needles that tell you exactly what they are best for right on the package. A universal needle works well for many fabrics, but you may want to switch to a denim needle when working with thick layers, a leather needle when working with leather or faux leather, and a microtex needle for delicate fabrics that require piercing of very fine or densely woven fabrics.

Having an assortment of needles in your sewing room will make sewing your project much easier. There are some things you should always remember, like replacing your sewing machine needle after every few projects or after eight to ten hours of sewing. A dull needle can cause skipped stitches, uneven stitches, or snagging.

techniques

STAYSTITCHING

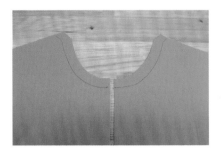

Staystitching is a line of stitching that stabilizes a curved edge, such as a neckline. This step is generally done first, before pieces are joined together. It's a simple line of machine stitching that is usually done about ⅛" away from the seamline.

UNDERSTITCHING

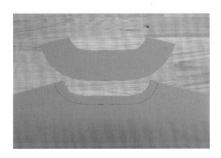

Understitching is a row of stitches that is sewn along the edge of a facing or lining. This row of stitches works to keep your facings or linings lying flat by sewing them to the seam allowance, which helps them fold neatly to the inside of your garment. You should also understitch pocket facings and waistband facings.

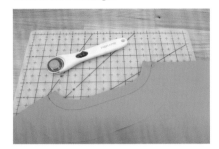

After stitching a facing in place, I like to trim my seam allowance to ⅜" and press the seam allowance towards the FACING, not the garment.

Make sure your seam allowance is still pressed towards your facing and stitch close to the seamline (about ⅛" away) through your facing and seam allowance.

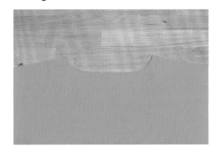

Press the facing or lining to the inside.

SEWING DARTS

A dart creates shaping in your garment. Some darts are straight with a single point, like bust darts or waist darts, while others may be curved or double-ended; you often see double-ended darts in sheath dresses or button-up shirts. They have two points, one at each end, with a wider section along the middle of the dart.

Here's my technique for a basic bust dart:

I first fully mark my dart on my fabric. Using a washable fabric marking pen I trace in both dart legs and also mark the center of the dart to the point.

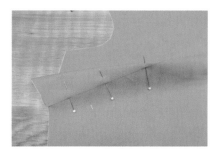

This allows me to fold my dart along the center line and accurately pin it in place.

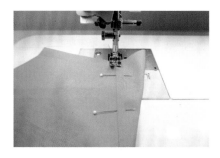

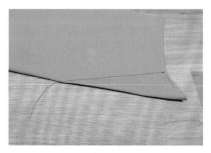

Sew along the dart leg until you reach the point, but do not back stitch—simply sew completely off your garment leaving long thread tails. Tie a double knot with the long threads. This will prevent you from getting a bubble at the point that is often seen when backstitching.

Using a tailors ham or a towel to help keep the shape of your dart, press your dart down.

GATHERING

Gathering is a technique that you will use on all types of garments. Gathering reduces the width of one piece of fabric so that you can join it to another piece that is smaller. You will see this often in full skirts, dresses, peplums, and sleeves.

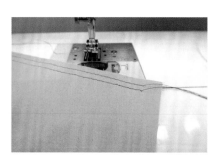

Start by changing the length of your stitch to the longest stitch available on your machine. Make two rows of stitching, both of which should be within your seam allowance. For example, if my seam allowance is ⅝" I will sew my first row at ⅛" and my second row ¼" inside the first row.

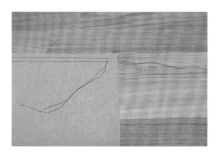

Make sure to backstitch at the beginning of each row but not at the end. Leave long thread tails and cut.

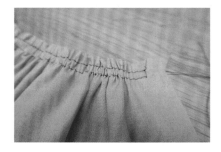

Grab your bobbin threads and pull to create gathers. Gather until your piece is the same width as the piece your plan to join it to.

Adjust your gathers evenly.

INSERTING ELASTIC

Elastic is used when making pull-on garments such as pants, dresses or skirts, and you will also see elastic in sleeve hems and pant hems—think casual pants like joggers.

There are several ways to insert elastic. In this book, several hacks have elasticized waists where the elastic is inserted into a casing, which is essentially a folded and stitched channel. A casing can be a separate piece or a self-casing, which is an extension of the garment piece that is simply folded over and stitched.

Start by cutting the elastic to your desired measurement, with a little extra for an overlap. Finish the raw edge of the casing by either serging or folding under ¼" and pressing, then fold the casing to meet the stitching line.

Pin in place and stitch close to the folded edge, leaving an opening of about 1½" to insert the elastic.

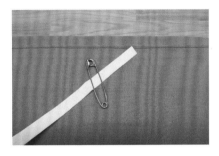

Using a safety pin, pin to one end of your elastic and insert into the opening; make sure to secure the free end of the elastic with a pin so it doesn't disappear inside the casing.

Use the safety pin to pull your elastic through until you reach the opening. Join the elastic with a few zigzag stitches, then push it fully inside the casing. Stitch your opening closed.

FLAT SLEEVE

Using this technique to attach a sleeve is one of my favorite methods. I find that I have more control when sewing the sleeve onto the armhole this way. Unlike a set-in sleeve, you do not sew the side seam of the bodice or the underarm seam of your sleeve first. This also allows for easier fitting since you don't need to remove your sleeve to adjust the side seam if needed.

Start by sewing two rows of gathering stitches within your seam allowance. Backstitch at one end but not the other.

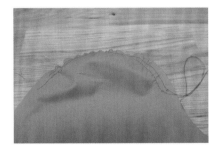

You will use your bobbin threads from the free end to ease your sleeve cap onto the armhole. Unlike gathering you will not be pulling to create folds but instead will just pull your threads to take up the ease without creating gathers in the sleeve cap.

Once you have eased the sleeve cap, start by pinning at your notches first, then your shoulder seam. Carefully pin the sleeve onto the armhole, making sure not to create folds or pleats. Adjust with the bobbin threads as needed and distribute evenly.

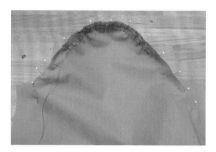

Note: If you find you still have too much ease you can create a series of snips into your bodice (not your sleeve cap)—the clips will help the fabric give a little as you need it. Sew your sleeve in place. Your sleeve should be free of any puckers when finished.

Once you have sewn your sleeve onto your armhole, place right sides together and pin along the side seam and sleeve. Sew side seams and sleeve.

SET-IN SLEEVE

As its name suggests, this sleeve is set into the armhole of the bodice before it is sewn in place. Unlike the flat sleeve technique, the sleeve and the bodice are sewn individually before the sleeve is "set" into the armhole. While I generally use the flat sleeve technique, you may prefer this one.

Start by sewing two rows of gathering stitches within your seam allowance. Backstitch at one end but not the other. You will use your bobbin threads to ease your sleeve cap onto the armhole.

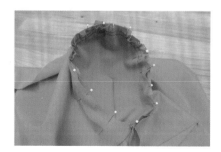

Pin your sleeve right sides facing to the armhole, making sure to pin first at your notches and shoulder and then pin in between those areas, easing your sleeve cap as needed. Stitch in place.

FLY FRONT

The fly front zipper is the most common zipper found in pants, denim skirts, trousers, and menswear. Oftentimes in patterns the fly extension is a separate piece that is sewn on, but many years ago I feel in love with Sandra Betzina's method so whenever I have a pattern that does not have a fly, I make one. But the patterns in this book have a built-in fly, so all you have to do is follow the instructions below to insert a great-looking zipper.

1. Start by interfacing the fly extensions; it's easiest to also serge or zigzag the front and back crotches before constructing. Place the front pieces right sides facing, pin, and stitch from the crotch to the hipline on the pant. From where you stopped stitching, switch to a basting length stitch and stitch all the way to the waist. (The line of basting is removed later).

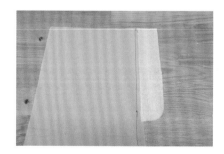

Clip into the seam allowance at the base of the fly, making sure not to cut through your stitching. Press the seam allowances and fly open.

2. Fold the pants RS together along the center seam, leaving one fly extended away from the garment. Be sure the other fly is folded back with the rest of the pants. With the zipper closed, place it RS down aligning one edge with the center front seam.

Stitch the opposite side of the zipper tape to the fly, sewing down the middle of the zipper tape.

Fold this extension under toward the pant, leaving the zipper now right side up, and topstitch along the exposed zipper teeth.

Flip the pants so the opposite fly is now extended and the other half of the zipper is lying flat on top.

Stitch it in place; none of this zipper stitching will be visible on the outside of the pant.

3. Turn the pants to the right side, with each fly folded flat in place. On the right pant leg, make a guideline with chalk or fabric pen 1¼" away from the seam, curving at the bottom below the zipper stop. Topstitch along the line, then remove the basting stitches.

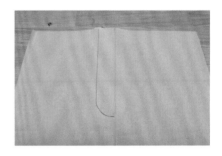

INVISIBLE ZIPPER

This technique creates a sleek result in a pant or a skirt. Installation instructions come with the zipper, but I have used an alternate method for the pencil skirt. See illustrations for this technique on page 48.

INTERFACING

Depending on the type of interfacing you use, it can be ironed on or sewn in. Generally speaking, interfacing is applied to a piece like a collar or cuff for stability or crispness and is added before the piece is fully constructed. Read more about interfacing on page 19.

choosing your size

The best way to pick the correct size on a pattern is to know your body measurements. This may seem difficult to do on your own, so if you have someone who can help you that would be best. If you don't have someone to help you, don't worry—you can still gather these measurements on your own. Here are some tips:

1. Wear a bra and underwear or leggings.
2. Tie a piece of elastic around the narrowest part of your waist. The elastic will naturally sit at the narrowest part of your waist. You could also place a finger along the side of your body at waist height and bend to either side—wherever that fold happens is your natural waist.
3. Stand up straight and face a mirror to make sure you are measuring in the correct places. This will also allow you to see the measurement in the mirror without shifting your body.
4. Make sure the measuring tape is always straight and level around your body.

HOW TO MEASURE YOUR BODY

1. Full Bust: Measure around your body at the fullest part of your bust.
2. Under Bust: Measure around your body under your bust at your ribcage.
3. Waist: Measure around your body at your waist where the elastic is naturally sitting.
4. Full Hip: Measure around your body at the fullest part of your buttocks.
5. Actual Hip: Measure around your body at your hip bone. You can generally feel for your hip bone with your fingers.
6. High Point Shoulder to Waist: Measure down to your waist from the point where your neck meets your shoulder, over your bust to the waist.
7. High Point Shoulder to Actual Hip: Measure down to your actual hip from the point where your neck meets your shoulder.
8. Waist to Knee: Measure down from waist to knee.
9. Inseam: It's probably easiest to take a pair of pants you own, that fit well, and measure the inside of the leg from the crotch to the hem.

SIZE CHART VERSUS FINISHED MEASUREMENTS

Below is the size conversion chart for the base patterns in the book. It is likely that your body measurements will not all fall within one size; for example, my waist falls in the medium column, but my hips fall in the large column. If that is the case for you the best way to choose your size is to look at the finished measurements given for the pattern. To be honest, I always look at the finished measurements of a pattern when given; they are often found in commercial patterns and most indie patterns. The finished garment measurements are the measurements of the actual garment once it is sewn. *(Finished garment measurements are included for each base pattern in this book.)*

Wearing ease is a personal choice, meaning I may like my dresses or pants to be more fitted than you prefer. Therefore, the finished garment measurements should be used as your guide to how that garment is going to fit after it is sewn up. This will tell you how much design ease was added to the pattern, and based on your body measurements and fit preference you can choose which size to cut.

Generally speaking, if you are making a shirt, blazer, or coat you may want to choose your pattern size based on your bust measurement, because it is easier to adjust at the waist and shoulder than at the bust. If you are making a fitted skirt with a waistband or elastic, you may want to choose based on your hip measurement and adjust at the waist. If you are making a very loose skirt or pants, then you would choose based on your waist measurement.

PATTERN SIZE	XXS	XS	S	M	L	XL	2XL
equivalent to :							
US	4	6	8	10	12–14	14–16	18–20
AUSTRALIAN/ UK	6	8	10	12	14–16	18–20	20–22
EU	32	34	36	38	40–42	44–46	46–48
Bust	81.5 cm 32"	86.5 cm 34"	91.5 cm 36"	96.5 cm 38"	104 cm 41"	112 cm 44"	119.5cm 47"
Natural Waist	61 cm 24"	66 cm 26"	71 cm 28"	76 cm 30"	84 cm 33"	91.5 cm 36"	99 cm 39"
Full Hip (20 cm below waist)	89 cm 35"	94 cm 37"	99 cm 39"	104 cm 41"	112 cm 44"	119.5 cm 47"	127 cm 50"

GRADING BETWEEN SIZES

All our bodies are different, and there isn't a pattern sold commercially that will fit all of us without having to make some sort of adjustment to the pattern. The most common adjustment made before the fitting process begins is grading between sizes. As I mentioned earlier, I often fall between a medium at the waist and a large at the hip; therefore, on a pant or skirt pattern, I grade between those two sizes by drawing a line from the medium waist to the large hip. Once that adjustment is made to the pattern front, I also make it to the back. You can also make the same adjustment to a bodice if you have a large bust and smaller or larger waist: simply draw a line from one size to the next.

It's best to draw your grading lines between notches at the points where you need a different size. You can easily grade between two and up to three different sizes. The fewer seamlines your garment has, the easier it is to grade, but even when there are several seamlines it is very doable and just requires that you make the same adjustments between notches to all the pattern pieces.

This the first step before cutting your pattern, but you may find that further adjustments are needed as you sew and fit. Fitting is something you will continuously learn, so I have included some of my favorite fitting resources in the Resources section (page 176).

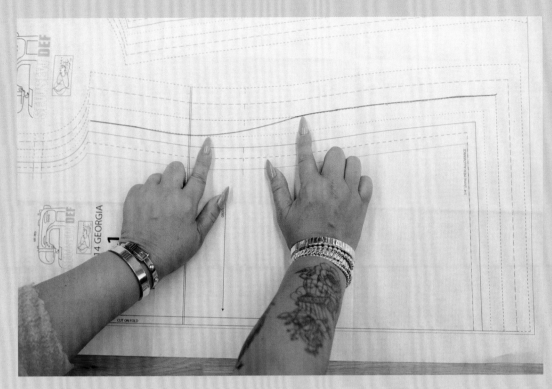

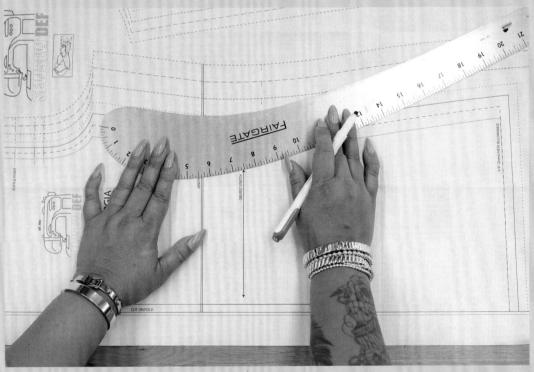

pattern know-how

PATTERN TERMS

Patterns are marked with all sorts of basic construction symbols to help you sew your garment together. The instructions in this book, much like in commercial patterns, go hand in hand with the markings on the actual pattern pieces to give you a complete guide to constructing your garment.

notches

Notches are your friend! They tell you where the pattern pieces are to be joined and sewn together. They are small lines or triangles along the cutting edge of your pattern pieces. Marking your notches is very important and will help you avoid making mistakes like joining two pieces together upside down or to the wrong pattern piece. This is helpful when working with a garment that has a lot of seamlines. You will generally find one or two notches next to each other at your center front or center back pattern pieces. On sleeve heads, two notches signify it is the back of the sleeve and one notch signifies it is the front of the sleeve.

darts

Darts are marked with a triangle with long legs, which are sewn together to create shaping. You will find darts in the bust and waist of some bodices, along with fisheye darts that start and end with points (like two regular darts set base-to-base). You will also find darts in the waist of pants and skirts.

placement marks

Placement markings are often used to mark where you will be placing pockets, flaps, and zippers. They also may be used to tell when to start and stop sewing. Different pattern companies use different markings, but most often they are circles in various sizes.

pleat markings

Pleat markings are usually two parallel lines with circles to align to finish the pleat. You may also see two parallel lines with an arrow that indicates the direction to bring the pleat lines together.

buttonhole and button marks

These markings indicate where you will be making a buttonhole and attaching your button.

grainline arrows

A grainline arrow is a very important marking because it tells you how to place your pattern piece onto your fabric. A woven fabric's grainline (or straight grain) runs parallel to the selvedge or "finished" edge, or along the yardage length. The cross grain runs parallel to the fabric's cut edge, or across the fabric's width. Bias grain runs at a 45-degree angle to the straight and cross grain and is often used to take advantage of a fabric's natural "give" or stretch. A grainline marking will also tell you if the pattern piece needs be placed on the cross grain or on the bias.

Knit fabrics do not have grainlines in the way woven fabrics do, but they do have directional stretch. If a pattern is designed for knit fabrics the grainline on the pattern pieces indicates the greatest stretch on your fabric.

LAYOUTS AND GRAINLINES

The one thing you don't want to do is waste fabric, so understanding the placement of a pattern on the fabric is very important. Your pattern pieces should be arranged according to the grainline and with consideration for which pattern pieces need to be placed on the fold of your fabric.

Consider the following when placing your pattern pieces:

- Make sure your fabric has no wrinkles; giving it a good press before laying out pattern pieces will assure you cut the piece accurately.
- If you have a large table, use it! It is so much easier to lay your fabric out and place your pattern pieces on a large surface. This also gives you an idea of how you can place the patterns to give you the best use of the fabric.
- Start with the largest pattern pieces first. Try your best to place pattern pieces that are the same length together. For example, place your bodice front and bodice back next to each other.
- Use the smaller pattern pieces to fill in empty spaces.

Every base pattern in the book has a fabric layout guide to help you place your patterns in the most economical way to get the most use of your fabric yardage.

TRACING PATTERNS

Now that you know what the pattern markings mean, you are ready to trace your pattern or print your PDF. Either way, you will be choosing your size based on your finished measurements as mentioned earlier. You will be starting with one of the base patterns, which is what we will use to create other styles. I suggest you follow the steps below to prep your base pattern.

1. Trace or print your pattern.

2. Choose your size based on the finished measurement chart given on each base pattern page. This will be the most accurate way of cutting the size that will fit best.

3. Make any grading adjustments on your pattern before you cut it out.

4. Cut your pattern following the cutting line of the size chosen or the new graded lines you've drawn.

5. Label each traced pattern clearly with the base pattern name and the size you cut.

getting ready to sew

CUT AND TEST YOUR BASE PATTERN

Cut your pattern out of muslin. This is strongly recommended so that you can test-fit the pattern before cutting into your fashion fabric. You can make fit adjustments like lengthening, shortening, letting out or taking in your side seams, and checking for an overall good fit on the muslin. The muslin is never a fully sewn garment; it is just sewn together to check for fit, so you don't have to attach collars, both sleeves, plackets, etc., but you want to make sure to sew in any darts. After making a muslin for fit testing you will want to mark the paper pattern with any adjustments you made for future use.

The order of construction and instructions are given for each base pattern to help you understand how to put the garment together. Complete instructions won't be given for each hack, though; instead I will cover the hacking steps and anything you may need to know that we did not already cover in the base pattern instructions.

LAYING OUT YOUR FABRIC

Fabric has a selvedge edge; it is the edge that runs the length of your fabric and looks different or "finished." You will fold your fabric in half with selvedge edges meeting. Place your pattern pieces according to the grainlines and cutting layout. If you are working with plaid or slippery fabrics, you may want to cut the pattern pieces twice on a single layer of fabric instead of cutting two at once with your fabric folded (remember to flip the pattern over when cutting the second piece—otherwise you will end up with two right back bodice pieces, for example).

Once you place your pattern pieces on your fabric you may choose to pin them to the fabric or use pattern weights. Pattern weights sold in stores are pricey and you only get six or so. I don't like to pin my pattern pieces, so I use my version of pattern weights, which are just large washers found at a home improvement store. Use plenty of weights so your pattern doesn't move as you cut. Using your scissors or rotary cutter, cut your fabric. Go slowly—you want accurate cuts without jagged edges. I find the rotary is better for getting clean cuts, but do what works best for you.

Before removing your pattern weights or pins, make sure to transfer ALL your markings. Using a chalk roller or marking pen, transfer any darts, buttonhole or button markings, and notches and take note of your seam allowance.

THE BASE PAT-TERNS

base patterns
sewing instructions

Before we start hacking our patterns to create our modifications, we first need to sew and fit our base patterns. The base patterns are the basic shapes I love and use often to create many different looks. If you are wondering if you need to be a math whiz, you can relax. Most of our modifications are done by slashing and spreading. This is an easy and fun way of creating multiple styles from one basic shape. It only requires that you begin with a good-fitting base pattern so you can avoid wasting time modifying a pattern only to find it doesn't fit.

GETTING STARTED

In this section I will be walking you though the sewing instructions for each base pattern in the book. Once the base pattern is printed or traced off, you will choose your size based on the size chart given for each base pattern. Grading between sizes at the waist or hip is very common and easy to do. Refer to the grading section of this book (page 28) for more information.

After selecting your base pattern size and tracing the pattern pieces in your size, cut your pattern pieces out and then cut them out of muslin to check fit. For your convenience, cutting layouts for each Base Pattern are on pages 172–175. Now I won't lie to you and say that I make muslins for everything I sew, because I don't. But if the pattern I am making is semi-fitted or fitted I tend to lean on the side of caution and will make a rough muslin so I can work out any fit issues I may have. I specifically do this for pants! Our bodies are shaped differently, so making a muslin will ensure that you end up with a good-fitting base to hack and modify.

One of the biggest benefits of making a muslin is your ability to adjust and write down any fit fixes you made to your muslin, and then you can transfer those changes to your paper pattern. The next time you go to make that pattern you won't need to worry about fit, unless your measurements have changed. I cover some of the more common fit issues and fixes in this book, but fitting is something you will continuously learn, so I have included some of my favorite fitting resources in the Resource section (see page 176).

Once you have made your muslin, made any adjustments you needed, and have transferred those to your base paper pattern, you can feel confident in using your adjusted pattern to make all the modifications shown in the book without concern for major fit issues.

AS YOU SEW

The Base Pattern instructions assume a certain level of sewing skill. Standard procedures such as applying interfacing may not appear in the instructions, so use the markings on the pattern piece to guide whether you need to apply interfacing to a particular piece. I also assume you know how to make buttonholes, stitch buttons on, and perform other basic sewing tasks; see Part One (page 21) for simple instructions for the standard techniques I use. I also recommend finishing all raw edges in the manner of your choice, such as serging, zigzagging, or folding under, so the inside of your garment looks as great as the outside! Finishing the raw edges also helps increase the durability of your garment.

BASE PATTERN:
the button-up

Fabric recommendations: Cottons, cotton blends, rayons or challis; see yardage chart, pages 64–65, and Cutting Layouts, page 172.

Notions: 10 ½" buttons, lightweight fusible interfacing

PATTERN PIECES:

- Front (Cut 2 main fabric)
- Back (Cut 1 main fabric on fold)
- Sleeve (Cut 2 main fabric)
- Back Yoke (Cut 2 main fabric on fold)
- Upper Collar (Cut 2 main fabric on fold/Cut 1 interfacing on fold; you can cut this from contrasting fabric if you like)
- Under Collar (Cut 2 main fabric on fold/Cut 1 interfacing on fold)
- Front Band (Cut 2 main fabric and 2 interfacing)
- Sleeve Cuff (Cut 2 main fabric and 2 interfacing; you can cut this from contrasting fabric if you like)
- Upper Sleeve Placket (Cut 2 main fabric)
- Under Sleeve Placket (Cut 2 main fabric)

SEAM ALLOWANCE:

- ⅜" (1 cm) unless otherwise noted.

STEP 1

Stitch the darts in the FRONT. Staystitch the neckline.

STEP 2

Fold along the BACK pleat lines so that each meets at center back. Baste along the top edge.
With RIGHT SIDES (RS) together, pin the BACK YOKE to the back. Stitch. Pin the FRONT to the BACK RS together at the shoulders. Stitch (A).

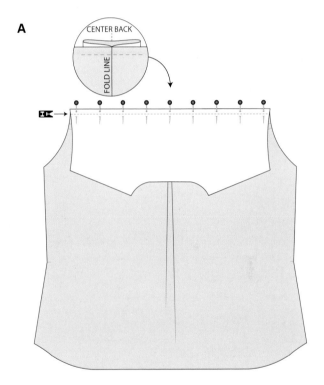

STEP 3

With your SLEEVE WRONG SIDE (WS) up, cut along the center of the placket box markings you transferred. The placket pieces will be sewn to the sleeve slit with the RS of the placket to the WS of the sleeve. The UNDER SLEEVE PLACKET should be placed on the side of the slit that is nearest the underarm seam on each sleeve.

As seen at the right, pin and stitch the UNDER SLEEVE PLACKET to the slit using a ¼" (6 mm) seam allowance and continue stitching to a ¼" above the slit (B).

With the needle down, align the UPPER SLEEVE PLACKET to the other half of the slit. Pivot, stitch across the top, stop ¼" past the cut edge, then pivot again and sew down the remaining side. Snip into the corners through all thicknesses. Snip as close to the stitches in the corner as possible but don't cut though them.

Press the resulting triangle up and turn everything to the RS of the sleeve. Press again.

Move the upper placket out of the way. Press the seam allowance on the under placket toward the placket. Press ¼" (6 mm) on the cut edge of the under placket to the placket's WS, then fold and press again so the first fold aligns to just past the stitching line. Edgestitch along the fold.

Working now with the upper placket, press the seam allowance toward the placket. Then fold the cut edge to WS by ¼" and press. Fold down and press the top of the upper placket to ¼" (6 mm). Fold in half with WS together, press, and place the folded edge just past the stitching line.

To finish the placket, start stitching it down from the bottom of the upper placket (where you folded and pressed the ¼" edge), stitch until you reach the top corner, pivot, stitch across the top, pivot again, and stitch down 1¼" (3 cm) and then pivot once more to stitch across the bottom to create the box. Press (C).

B

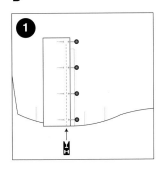
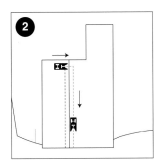
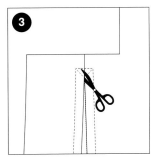
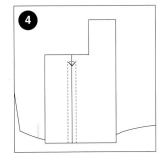

C

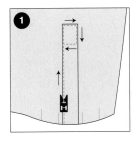
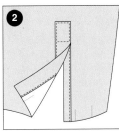
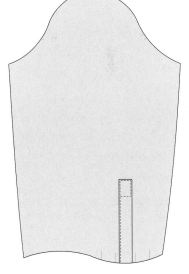

STEP 4

Make two rows of gathering stitches on the sleeve cap from notch to notch and pull the bobbin threads slightly to ease the sleeve cap. Attach the sleeve flat by pinning first at the front and back notches, then pin at the shoulder seam notch and ease the sections in between. Pin, then stitch.

STEP 5

Now that the sleeves are attached, let's sew up the side seam and underarm seam. With RS together, pin along the entire sleeve and down the side seam. Stitch using ⅜" (1 cm) seam allowance in one continuous seam, pivoting at the under arm.

STEP 6

Sew the hem of the shirt by serging the raw edge and turning under the ⅝" (1.5 cm) hem allowance or making a double fold of ¼" (6 mm) and then ⅜" (1 cm). Stitch.

STEP 7

Pin the FRONT BAND to each of the shirt's front edges, RS together and matching the notch. Stitch using ⅜" (1 cm) seam allowance. On the free edge of the band, press ⅜" (1 cm) to WS, then press the band WS together along the center foldline, making sure the first folded edge aligns just past the stitching line. Stitch close to the folded edge.

STEP 8

Place the UPPER COLLAR pieces RS together. Pin, then stitch using ⅜" (1 cm) seam allowance along the short sides and top. Clip the corners and turn RS out. Press. Topstitch ⅜" (1 cm) from the edge.

STEP 9

On the non-interfaced UNDER COLLAR, press ⅜" (1 cm) to WS along the bottom edge. Sandwich the sewn collar between the under collar band pieces, RS together and matching notches. Stitch from one rounded edge of the under collar to the opposite, leaving the bottom edge unsewn, and turn RS out. Press the constructed collar (D).

D

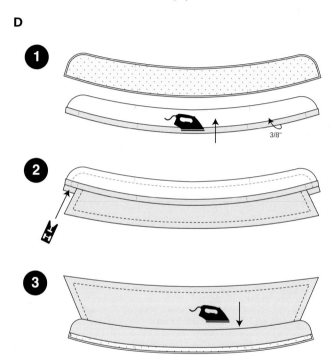

STEP 10

Pin the raw edge of the collar onto the right side of the shirt neckline, matching notches and clipping into the curves as needed. Stitch and press to the inside. Finish the collar by hand slipstitching the non-interfaced collar band's folded edge to the stitching line, or pin it in place and stitch in the ditch from the RS, catching the folded edge in the stitches.

STEP 11

Make the pleats on your sleeve hem as indicated by the pleat lines on your pattern. Press one long edge of the SLEEVE CUFF to WS by ⅜" (1 cm), then fold along the foldline with RS together. Stitch the cuff along the short ends, turn RS out, and press. Pin the cuff onto the sleeve, RS together, then stitch, leaving the folded edge free. Now place the folded edge on the WS just past the stitching line, pin, and stitch in the ditch from the RS. Try on the shirt and decide where to make the button-holes on the right front band. Make buttonholes on the sleeve cuff and front band and sew on your buttons to the left front band (E).

E

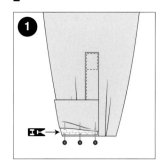
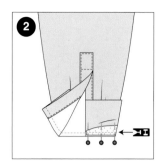

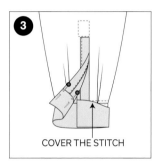
COVER THE STITCH

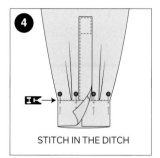
STITCH IN THE DITCH

FINISHED GARMENT MEASUREMENTS

PATTERN SIZE	XXS	XS	S	M	L	XL	2XL
BUST	94 cm 37"	99 cm 39"	104 cm 41"	109 cm 43"	116.5 cm 46"	124 cm 49"	131.5 cm 52"
WAIST	82 cm 32¼"	87 cm 34¼"	92 cm 36¼"	97 cm 38¼"	104.5 cm 41¼"	112 cm 44¼"	119.5 cm 47¼"
HIPS	100 cm 39¼"	105 cm 41¼"	110 cm 43¼"	115 cm 45¼"	122.5 cm 48¼"	130 cm 51¼"	137.5 cm 54¼"
BICEP	33.5 cm 13¼"	35.5 cm 14"	37.5 cm 14¾"	39.5 cm 15¾"	42.5 cm 16¾"	45.5 cm 18"	48.5 cm 19⅛"

BASE PATTERN:
the trousers

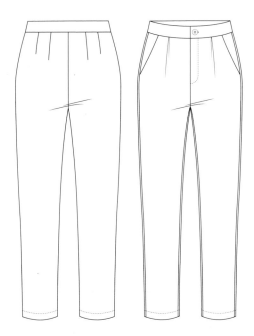

Fabric recommendations: Bottom weights, cotton blends, lightweight denims, twills, gabardine; see yardage chart, pages 64–65, and Cutting Layouts, page 172.

Notions: 1 ¾" button, lightweight fusible interfacing, 9" zipper

PATTERN PIECES:

*   Front (Cut 2 main fabric)
*   Back (Cut 2 main fabric)
*   Pocket Bag (Cut 2 main fabric)
*   Pocket Facing (Cut 2 main fabric)
*   Waistband (Cut 1 main fabric and 1 interfacing)
*   Belt Loop (Cut 1 main fabric)

SEAM ALLOWANCE:

*   ⅜" (1 cm) unless otherwise noted

STEP 1

Interface the fly extensions. Serge or zigzag the FRONT and BACK crotches before constructing. With RIGHT SIDES (RS) together, pin the two fronts at the crotch. Stitch using a ⅜" (1 cm) seam allowance from the end of the crotch to the hipline marked on the pattern and backstitch. From where you stopped stitching, switch to a basting stitch and begin stitching again all the way up toward the waist (this stitching will be removed later). Clip into the seam allowance, making sure not cut through your stitching, at the base of the fly. Press the seam allowances and fly open (A).

A

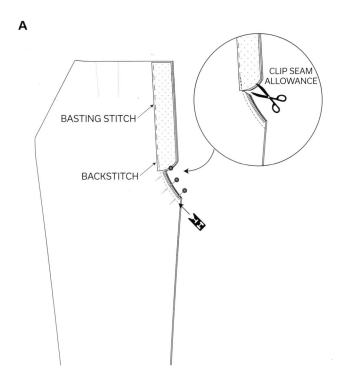

STEP 2

See the Techniques section to continue the fly-front zipper installation step (page 24); begin with step 2.

STEP 3

Make the pleats in the front of your pants by bringing the pleat lines together as marked on the pattern. Sew the darts on the back of the pants. Press them toward center back (B).

STEP 4

Pin the POCKET FACING to the front pant, RS together and matching notches. Stitch using ⅜" (1 cm) seam allowance, then press out and understitch the facing. Turn the pocket facing to inside and press. Pin the POCKET BAG to pocket facing, RS together and making sure everything is lying flat. Stitch the pocket bag to the pocket facing. Stitch the pocket bag to the pants front along the waist and side seam to secure (C).

STEP 5

With RS together, pin and stitch the back crotch. Press seam allowances open.

STEP 6

Place the pants front RS together with pants back and pin the inseams and side seams. Stich using ⅜" (1 cm) seam allowance. Turn the pants RS out and press. Press under the hems and sew with a straight stitch or use a blind hem.

B

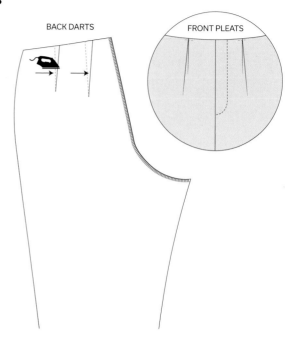

BACK DARTS

FRONT PLEATS

C

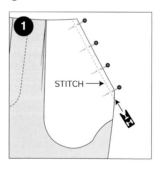

STITCH →

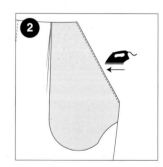

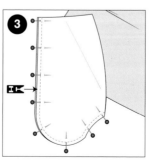

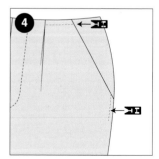

STEP 7

Press ⅜" (1 cm) along one long edge of the WAISTBAND. Pin the other edge to the pants waist, matching marks. The ends of the waistband extend past the front fly on each end. Stitch. To finish the front ends of the waistband, fold the waistband's short ends RS together and stitch. Clip the corners and turn RS out (D).

STEP 8

Fold the waistband along the foldline and press, making sure the bottom folded edge on the inside of the pants is just past the stitching line. Pin the waistband in place on WS and stitch in the ditch from the RS (E).

STEP 9

If you want to add belt loops: Fold the piece in half WRONG SIDE (WS) facing, stitch using ⅜" (1 cm) seam allowance. Turn RS out and press. Decide how tall you want your belt loops to be and cut the piece into equal parts accordingly. Using a favorite belt as a guide might be helpful! Attach belt loops to waistband by turning under ⅜" (1 cm) on each end and topstitching through all layers. Make your buttonhole following your sewing machine instruction guide and sew on a button.

D

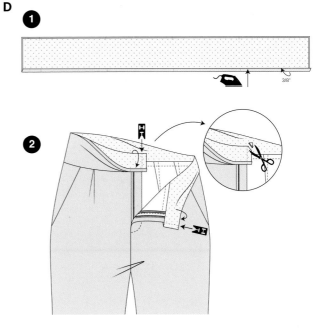

E

FINISHED GARMENT MEASUREMENTS

PATTERN SIZE	XXS	XS	S	M	L	XL	2XL
WAIST	61 cm 24"	66 cm 26"	71 cm 28"	76 cm 30"	83.5 cm 33"	91 cm 36"	98.5 cm 39"
HIPS	94 cm 37"	99 cm 39"	104 cm 41"	109 cm 43"	116.5 cm 46"	124 cm 49"	131.5 cm 52"
INSIDE LEG LENGTH	71 cm 28"	71 cm 28"	71 cm 28"	71 cm 28"	71 cm 28"	71 cm 28"	71 cm 28"

BASE PATTERN:
the pencil skirt

Fabric recommendations: Bottom weights, lightweight denims, twills, gabardine, stretch wovens; see yardage chart, pages 64–65, and Cutting Layouts, page 173.

Notions: Lightweight fusible interfacing, 14" invisible zipper

PATTERN PIECES:

- Front (Cut 1 main fabric on fold)
- Back (Cut 2 main fabric)
- Waistband (Cut 1 main fabric and 1 interfacing)

SEAM ALLOWANCE:

- ⅜" (1 cm) unless otherwise noted

STEP 1

Make darts in the FRONT and BACK skirt pieces.

STEP 2

Finish the edges of the back vent. With right sides (RS) together, stitch the two back pieces from the center back notch down to ⅝" (1.5 cm) past the vent's top edge, then pivot and stitch across the top of the vent. Clip to the corner of the vent (A). Fold the vent to one side or the other (it doesn't really matter which) and press well. Pin the vent in place. Working from the wrong side of the skirt, add another line of stitching on top of the existing seamline at the top of the vent; this will hold it in place (B).

A

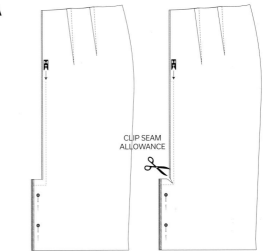

CLIP SEAM ALLOWANCE

B

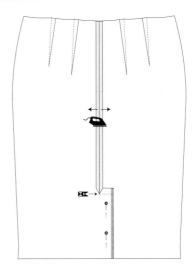

STEP 3

Place the front skirt to back skirt with RS together and pin both side seams. Stitch (C).

STEP 4

Fold the waistband in half along the foldline, wrong sides (WS) together, and press well. Then press one long edge of the WAISTBAND ⅜" (1 cm) to WS. Pin the other edge to the skirt, matching the notches to the center front; one end of the waistband is longer than the other to use in different projects, so trim away the longer edge so it is even with the skirt. Stitch and press the seam open. With RS together, baste the back seam from the pressed fold in the waistband to the hem, using a ⅝" seam, making sure that the waistline seams match. Press the seam allowance open.

STEP 5

To install the invisible zipper, place the closed zipper face down on the seam, with the top zipper stops aligned with the fold of the waistband. Pin the zipper to secure the placement, then hand baste it in place to the seam allowance only, unzipping as needed. Mark the zipper about 2½" above the bottom stop so you can stitch the back seam below the zipper. Fold the skirt so the back pieces are RS together, transfer the mark from the zipper to the skirt, and stitch from the mark to the hem, backstitching at both ends of the seam. You can stitch right on top of your line of basting (D).

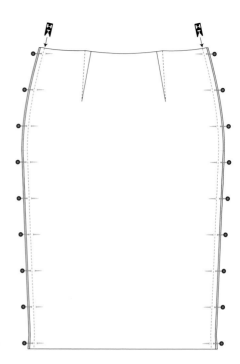

C

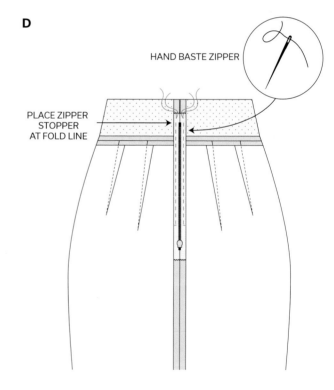

D

HAND BASTE ZIPPER

PLACE ZIPPER STOPPER AT FOLD LINE

E

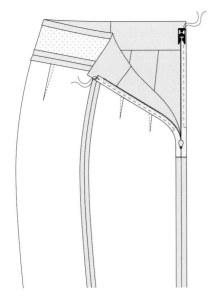

STEP 6

Remove the line of basting stitches above the mark, opening up the rest of the seam. Install the invisible zipper foot on your sewing machine and unzip the zipper completely. The zipper tape should be at the edge of the seam allowance. Stitch one side in place, stopping at the marked spot; repeat for the other side. Close the zipper after sewing it in place and check to make sure that your waistband seam still meets evenly. Remove the hand basting. Because the zipper is stitched to the seam allowances, you don't need to secure it at the bottom (E).

STEP 7

Fold the waistband RS together, folding the top of the zipper tape under at the stop and tucking it to the outside. Stitch the short ends close to the zipper. Turn RS out and push out the corners. Fold the waistband WS together and press, making sure the lower finished edge rests just past the stitching line. Pin the waistband in place and stitch in the ditch from RS.

F

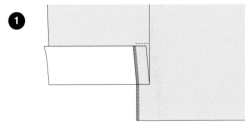

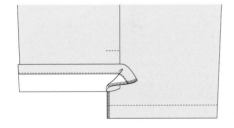

STEP 8

Before you hem the skirt, finish the raw edges. Here is a little trick to use for the back vent overlap so it is nice and neat: Open up the vent before you press up the hem allowance, then fold up the 1¼" (3 cm) hem allowance all the way around the skirt. Stitch the hem all the way around and fold the vent back in place. Tack the vent to the hem with a few stitches (F).

FINISHED GARMENT MEASUREMENTS

PATTERN SIZE	XXS	XS	S	M	L	XL	2XL
WAIST	61 cm 24"	66 cm 26"	71 cm 28"	76 cm 30"	83.5 cm 33"	91 cm 36"	98.5 cm 39"
HIPS	91 cm 35¼"	96 cm 37¼"	101 cm 39¼"	106 cm 41¼"	113.5 cm 44¼"	121 cm 47¼"	128.5 cm 50¼"

BASE PATTERN:
the fitted tee

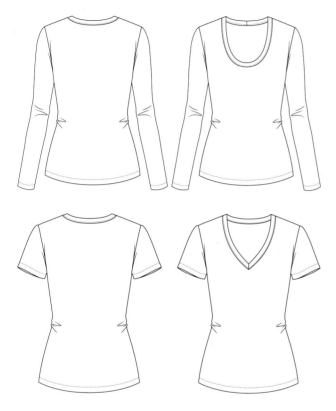

Fabric recommendations: Two-way stretch knits, jerseys, rib knits; see yardage chart, pages 64–65, and Cutting Layouts, page 173.

PATTERN PIECES:
- Front (Cut 2 main fabric on fold)
- Back (Cut 2 main fabric on fold)
- Sleeve (Cut 2 main fabric)
- Neckband (Cut 1 main fabric)

SEAM ALLOWANCE:
- ¼" (6 mm) unless otherwise noted

STEP 1

With RIGHT SIDES (RS) together, pin the FRONT to the BACK at the shoulders. Stitch. Press the seam allowances to one side. (If you like the cropped look in the photo, trim the front and back to your desired length now, leaving a ¾" [2 cm] hem allowance.)

STEP 2

Pin each SLEEVE into the armhole, RS together, making sure to pin it at the front, back, and shoulder notches. Ease the sleeve into the armhole by stretching slightly as needed. Stitch using a ¼" (6 mm) seam allowance (A). (This is the flat sleeve technique described on page 23.)

A

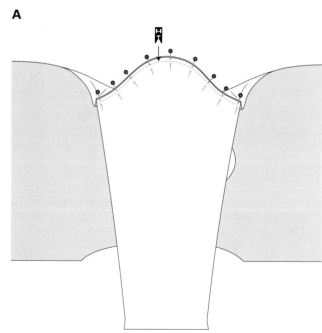

STEP 3

Pin along the sleeve underarm and tee side seams. Stitch in a continuous seam, using a ¼" (6 mm) seam allowance (B).

B

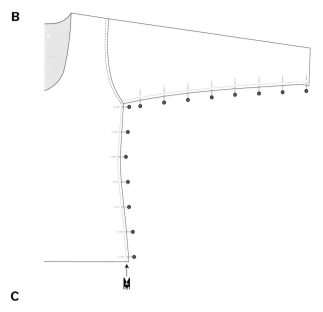

STEP 4

With the NECKBAND's short ends RS together, stitch and press the seam allowances open. (If you're using the V-neck band, it may be helpful to stitch in two steps, from center of the V out to one edge, then the other, to prevent stretching.) Fold the neckband in half and press. For the round neckline: With RS together, place the center back seam of the band on the center back of the tee neckline and pin the center front of the band to the center front of the tee neckline. Ease the band between shoulder and center back by stretching slightly to match neckline, and pin. Stitch using ¼" (6 mm) seam allowance (C). Press the band away from the neckline; understitch or topstitch as desired.

For the V neckline: staystitch the front neckline a few inches each way from the V for stability, and do the same to the band, trimming the seam as needed. Clip the V neckline just to the line of staystitching. Carefully pin the band with RS together, making sure the center of the neckline matches the center of the band. Then pin the rest of the band to the neckline, spreading the fabric at the clip, and stitch as the round neckline.

C

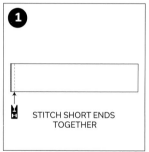

STITCH SHORT ENDS TOGETHER

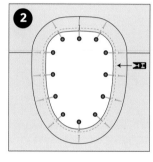

STEP 5

Press under the tee hem ¾" (2 cm) and stitch.

FINISHED GARMENT MEASUREMENTS

PATTERN SIZE	XXS	XS	S	M	L	XL	2XL
BUST	76 cm 29¾"	81 cm 31¾"	86 cm 33¾"	91 cm 35¾"	98.5 cm 38¾"	106 cm 41¾"	113.5 cm 44¾"
WAIST	74 cm 29"	79 cm 31"	84 cm 33"	89 cm 35"	96.5 cm 38"	104 cm 41"	111.5 cm 44"
HIPS	82 cm 32¼"	87 cm 34¼"	92 cm 36¼"	97 cm 38¼"	104.5 cm 41¼"	112 cm 44¼"	119.5 cm 47¼"
BICEP	27 cm 10¾"	29 cm 11½"	31 cm 12¼"	33 cm 13"	36 cm 14¼"	39 cm 15½"	41 cm 16¾"

BASE PATTERN:
the camisole

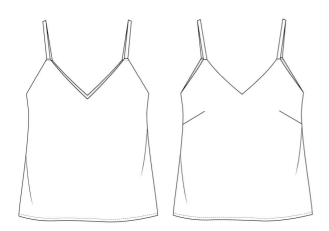

Fabric recommendations: Rayons, cotton blends, silky types; see yardage chart, pages 64–65, and Cutting Layouts, page 172.

PATTERN PIECES:

- Front (Cut 1 main fabric)
- Back (Cut 1 main fabric)
- Front Facing (Cut 1 main fabric and 1 interfacing)
- Back Facing (Cut 1 main fabric and 1 interfacing)
- Straps (Cut 2 main fabric)

SEAM ALLOWANCE:

- ⅜" (1 cm) unless otherwise noted

STEP 1

Sew the darts on the FRONT. With RIGHT SIDES (RS) together, place the front to BACK and stitch side seams. Press the seam allowances open (A).

STEP 2

With FRONT FACING and BACK FACING RS together, stitch the side seams. Press the seam allowances open.

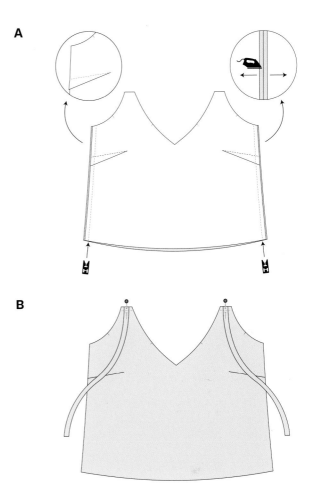

STEP 3

Fold the STRAPS in half lengthwise, with RS together. Sew using a ⅜" (1 cm) seam allowance, then turn RS out and press flat.

STEP 4

Pin the straps to the front and tack in place. *Do not* sew the other end of the strap to the back yet (B). Place the assembled facing over the camisole, RS together, and stitch, matching notches. Stitch across the straps on the front but leave the back of the straps free (C). Understitch the facing as far as possible and clip into the curves. Turn the facing to the inside and press.

C

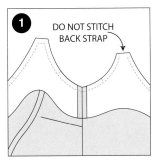

1 DO NOT STITCH BACK STRAP

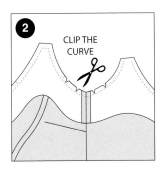

2 CLIP THE CURVE

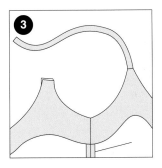

3

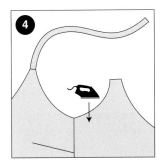

4

STEP 5

Now attach a safety pin to the back end of the strap and insert it into the back strap opening, between the camisole and the back facing. Pin it in place, turning under the raw edges, and try on the camisole. Adjust the strap as needed and then stitch the openings closed (D).

STEP 6

Since the cami is cut on the bias, allow it to hang for twenty-four hours to relax before hemming. Press the hem to the WRONG SIDE (WS) by ¼" (6 mm) and then again by ⅜" (1 cm) and stitch close to the folded edge.

D

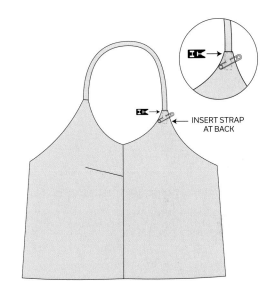

INSERT STRAP AT BACK

FINISHED GARMENT MEASUREMENTS

PATTERN SIZE	XXS	XS	S	M	L	XL	2XL
BUST	86 cm 33¾"	91 cm 35¾"	96 cm 37¾"	101 cm 39¾"	108.5 cm 42¾"	116 cm 45¾"	123.5 cm 48¾"
WAIST	87 cm 34¼"	92 cm 36¼"	97 cm 38¼"	102 cm 40¼"	109.5 cm 43¼"	117 cm 46¼"	124.5 cm 49¼"
HIPS	92 cm 36¼"	97 cm 38¼"	102 cm 40¼"	107 cm 42¼"	114.5 cm 45¼"	122 cm 48¼"	129.5 cm 51¼"

BASE PATTERN:
the wrap dress

Fabric recommendations: Two-way stretch knits, jerseys, rib knits; see yardage chart, pages 64–65, and Cutting Layouts, page 174.

PATTERN PIECES:

- Front Bodice (Cut 2 main fabric)
- Back Bodice (Cut 1 main fabric on fold)
- Skirt Front and Back (Front – cut 2 main fabric; Back - cut 1 main fabric on fold)
- Left Side Tie (Cut 1 main fabric)
- Right Side Tie (Cut 1 main fabric)
- Neck Binding (Cut 1 main fabric)
- Sleeve (Cut 2 main fabric)

SEAM ALLOWANCE:

- ¼" (6 mm) unless otherwise noted

STEP 1

Stitch darts in the FRONT BODICE. With RIGHT SIDES (RS) together, place the FRONT BODICE to the BACK BODICE at the shoulders and stitch. Press the seam allowances to one side.

STEP 2

Pin each SLEEVE into the armhole, making sure to pin at the front, back, and shoulder notches. Ease the sleeve in by stretching slightly as needed. Stitch using a ¼" (6 mm) seam allowance (A). (This is the flat sleeve technique described on page 23.)

A

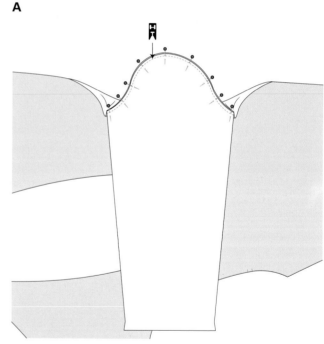

STEP 3

Pin along the sleeve underarm and bodice side seams. On one side, leave a 1″ (2.5 cm) opening ½″ (1.3 cm) above the waist for the waist tie to be inserted when wearing. Backstitch to secure above and below the opening. Stitch using ¼″ (6 mm) seam allowance (B).

B

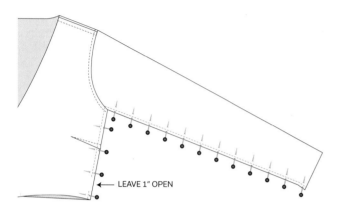

← LEAVE 1″ OPEN

STEP 4

Pin the NECK BINDING to the neckline, RS together, and stitch using a ¼″ (6 mm) seam allowance. Press under ¼″ (6 mm) on the opposite edge of the binding, then press binding to the inside. Stitch close to the neck binding's folded edge (C).

STEP 5

Pin the SKIRT FRONTS to the SKIRT BACK at the side seams with RS together. Stitch. Pin the skirt to the bodice with RS together and stitch using ¼″ (6 mm) seam allowance (D).

C

1/4″

STITCH CLOSE TO BINDING EDGE

D

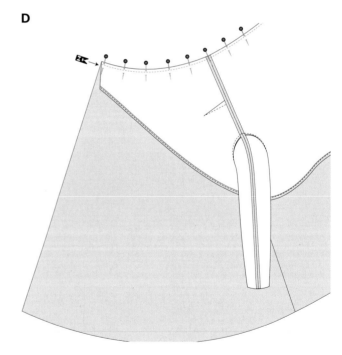

STEP 6

Fold the LEFT SIDE TIE in half lengthwise, RS together, pin, and stitch along the tie's long edge and angled short end. Turn RS out. Repeat for the RIGHT SIDE TIE (E).

E

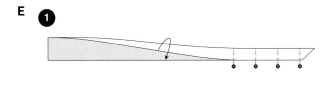

STEP 7

Pin the ties to the corresponding side of the dress front above the waist, RS together, aligning the cut edge of the tie and the front edge of the bodice. Tack in place. Fold and press the seam allowance to WRONG SIDE (WS) along the entire front bodice and the skirt edges, but be sure to finish the raw edges in your preferred manner before you stitch the seam allowance down, which will secure the ties in the process. Press the hem allowance ¾" (2 cm) to WS and stitch (F).

F

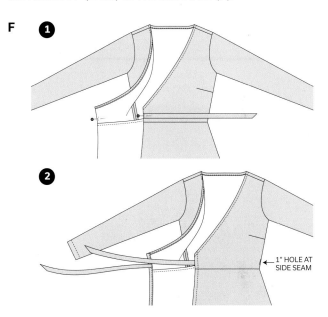

1" HOLE AT SIDE SEAM

FINISHED GARMENT MEASUREMENTS

PATTERN SIZE	XXS	XS	S	M	L	XL	2XL
BUST	77 cm 30¼"	82 cm 32¼"	87 cm 34¼"	92 cm 36¼"	99.5 cm 39¼"	117 cm 42¼"	124.5 cm 45¼"
WAIST	59 cm 23¼"	64 cm 25¼"	69 cm 27¼"	74 cm 29¼"	81.5 cm 32¼"	89 cm 35"	96.5 cm 38"
HIPS	100 cm 39¼"	105 cm 41¼"	110 cm 43¼"	115 cm 45¼"	122.5 cm 48"	130 cm 51¼"	137.5 cm 54¼"
BICEP	33.5 cm 13¼"	35.5 cm 14"	37.5 cm 14¾"	39.5 cm 15¾"	42.5 cm 16¾"	45.5 cm 18"	48.5 cm 19⅛"

BASE PATTERN:
the duster

Fabric recommendations: Pre-quilted fabrics, wools, denim, flannels. For a soft flowing Duster, use rayons, silky types; see yardage chart, pages 64–65, and Cutting Layouts, page 175.

PATTERN PIECES:

- Front (Cut 2 main fabric)
- Back (Cut 1 main fabric on fold)
- Sleeve (Cut 2 main fabric)
- Pocket (Cut 4 main fabric)
- Belt (Cut 2 main fabric)
- Neckband (Cut 2 main fabric and 2 interfacing)

SEAM ALLOWANCE:

- ⅜" (1 cm) unless otherwise noted

STEP 1

With RIGHT SIDES (RS) together, pin the FRONT to the BACK at the shoulders and stitch. Press the seam allowances to one side.

STEP 2

Pin the SLEEVE to the duster, RS together and matching the shoulder notch to the shoulder seam. Stitch. Press the seam allowances toward the sleeve (A). (This is the flat sleeve technique described on page 23.)

A

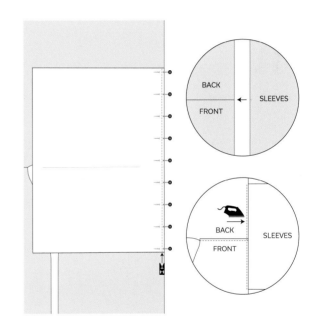

STEP 3

Pin each POCKET to the fronts and the back at the side seams, RS together and matching notches, and stitch. Press the pockets toward the seam allowances, RS out (B).

STEP 4

Pin along the sleeve underarm and the duster side seams, pinning the pocket pieces together at the edges. Stitch using a ⅜" (1 cm) seam allowance, starting at the duster hem and ending ¾" (2 cm) above the bottom of the pocket opening. Backstitch and cut the thread. Stitch around the edges of the pocket, ending ¾" (2 cm) below the top of the pocket opening and back-stitching. Begin stitching the side seam again 1" (2.5 cm) down from the top of the pocket to the under-arm and pivot, continuing to stitch along the sleeve underarm (C).

STEP 5

Press up the 1¼" (3 cm) hem allowance on the bottom hem and the sleeves and stitch.

B

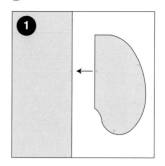
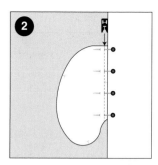
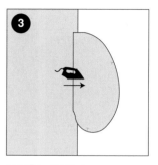

C

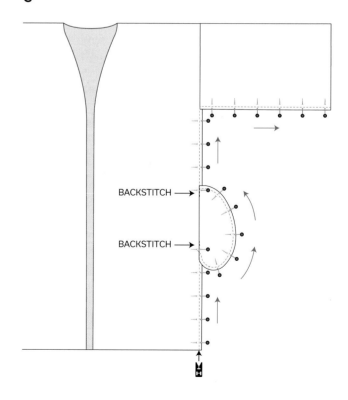

STEP 6

Pin and stitch the two NECKBAND pieces RS together at the center back seam. Press the seam allowances open. Fold the neckband in half lengthwise, WS together, and pin to the duster neckline, matching the center back and front notches. At the hem, fold the neckband RS together onto itself and stitch along the bottom, making sure it's even with the hem. Continue pinning. Stitch, starting at the center back and sewing down one front neckline, then start again at the center back and stitch down the other front. Press the neckband toward the seam allowances, RS out. Finish the raw edges using your favorite method (D).

STEP 7

If you want a belt: With the BELT pieces RS together at one short end, stitch, then press the seam allowances open. Fold the belt in half lengthwise, RS together. Stitch along both short ends and then along the length, making sure to leave a 1″ (2.5 cm) opening. Turn the belt RS out through the opening. Push out the corners and slipstitch the 1″ (2.5 cm) opening closed.

D

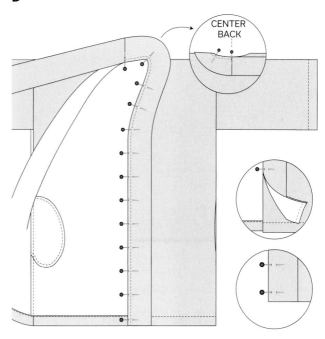

FINISHED GARMENT MEASUREMENTS

PATTERN SIZE	XXS	XS	S	M	L	XL	2XL
BUST	124 cm 48¾″	129 cm 50¾″	134 cm 52¾″	139 cm 54¾″	146.5 cm 57¾″	154 cm 60¾″	161.5 cm 63¾″
WAIST	124 cm 48¾″	129 cm 50¾″	134 cm 52¾″	139 cm 54¾″	146.5 cm 57¾″	154 cm 60¾″	161.5 cm 63¾″
HIPS	124 cm 48¾″	129 cm 50¾″	134 cm 52¾″	139 cm 54¾″	146.5 cm 57¾″	154 cm 60¾″	161.5 cm 63¾″

yardage charts

THE BUTTON-UP

PATTERN SIZE	XXS	XS	S	M	L	XL	2XL
115 cm / 45"	1.60 m 1¾ yards	1.70 m 1⅞ yards	1.80 m 2 yards	2.10 m 2¼ yards	2.10 m 2¼ yards	2.20 m 2⅜ yards	2.20 m 2⅜ yards
150 cm / 60"	1.20 m 1⅜ yards	1.20 m 1⅜ yards	1.30 m 1⅜ yards	1.40 m 1⅝ yards	1.50 m 1⅝ yards	1.60 m 1¾ yards	1.60 m 1¾ yards

THE TROUSERS

PATTERN SIZE	XXS	XS	S	M	L	XL	2XL
115 cm / 45"	1.85 m 2 yards	1.90 m 2⅛ yards	2 m 2¼ yards	2 m 2¼ yards	2.10 m 2¼ yards	2.20 m 2⅜ yards	2.20 m 2⅜ yards
150 cm / 60"	1.30 m 1⅜ yards	1.40 m 1⅝ yards	1.60 m 1¾ yards	2.0 m 2¼ yards	2.10 m 2¼ yards	2.20 m 2¼ yards	1.40 m 2⅜ yards

THE PENCIL SKIRT

PATTERN SIZE	XXS	XS	S	M	L	XL	2XL
115 cm / 45"	.80 m ⅞ yards	.80 m ⅞ yards	.90 m 1 yards	.90 m 1 yards	1.40 m 1⅝ yards	1.40 m 1⅝ yards	1.40 m 1⅝ yards
150 cm / 60"	.80 m ⅞ yards	.80 m ⅞ yards	.80 m ⅞ yards	.80 m ⅞ yards	.80 m ⅞ yards	.80 m ⅞ yards	.80 m ⅞ yards

THE FITTED TEE

PATTERN SIZE	XXS	XS	S	M	L	XL	2XL
150 cm / 60"	.80 m ⅞ yards	.80 m ⅞ yards	.80 m ⅞ yards	1.30 m 1⅜ yards	1.35 m 1⅜ yards	1.40 m 1⅝ yards	1.40 m 1⅝ yards

THE CAMISOLE

PATTERN SIZE	XXS	XS	S	M	L	XL	2XL
115 cm / 45"	.80 m 1 yards	.90 m 1 yards	1.0 m 1⅛ yards	1.10 m 1⅛ yards	1.20 m 1⅜ yards	1.30 m 1⅜ yards	1.30 m 1⅜ yards
150 cm / 60"	.70 m ¾ yards	.70 m ¾ yards	.75 m ⅞ yards	.80 m ⅞ yards	.90 m 1 yards	1.0 m 1⅛ yards	1.0 m 1⅛ yards

THE WRAP DRESS

PATTERN SIZE	XXS	XS	S	M	L	XL	2XL
150 cm / 65"	2.15 m 2⅜ yards	2.20 m 2⅜ yards	2.20 m 2⅜ yards	2.30 m 2½ yards	2.30 m 2½ yards	2.30 m 2½ yards	2.40 m 2⅝ yards

THE DUSTER

PATTERN SIZE	XXS	XS	S	M	L	XL	2XL
115 cm / 45"	2.75 m 3 yards	2.85 m 3⅛ yards	2.95 m 3¼ yards	3.0 m 3¼ yards	3.10 m 3⅜ yards	3.30 m 3⅝ yards	3.40 m 3¾ yards
150 cm / 60"	2.10 m 2¼ yards	2.20 m 2⅜ yards	2.30 m 2½ yards	2.40 m 2⅝ yards	2.50 m 2¾ yards	2.60 m 3 yards	2.60 m 3 yards

THE HACKS

let's create new patterns!

I really want you to keep in mind that these modifications have some element of personal choice. For instance, you can decide the length you want for any dress, skirt, pant hem, or top. Just because I am using a specific measurement for my length doesn't mean you have to use the same length. This is about your personal preference, so don't be afraid to customize.

Before getting started with modifying your patterns, let me share a few tips to help you along the way.

- Trace the pattern piece you are going to modify onto new paper. You don't want to modify the original pattern because you will use it again. Keep your base pattern intact.
- When laying your base pattern onto new paper, make sure you leave yourself a few inches above and below the pattern for tracing.
- Always start with a straight line drawn on your paper. This will be very important when slashing and spreading.
- Use an awl to punch out the pattern's dart point to make it easier to transfer the marking.
- Use a pencil to draw in cutting lines and colored pencils to mark fit changes, adjustments, or corrections. This will make it easy to identity anything that you need to remember before cutting your pattern.

BASIC PATTERN DRAFTING

You will be using simple techniques to create each hack in this section. It's not rocket science! But it does require care and precision. Here are brief explanations of the main patternmaking terms used in the instructions:

- Slash and spread. Cutting the pattern piece at a specific spot and then spreading the pattern to add volume and change the silhouette.
- Blend. Smoothing seamlines between altered pattern pieces by redrawing. May also be referred to as "truing."
- Square off. Corners or intersections need to be at 90-degree angles to meet accurately during construction.

For each hack, you will see a diagram that is keyed to the instructions. The numbers in grey circles on the diagram correspond to the step numbers.

CALCULATING FABRIC REQUIREMENTS

Because you're making your own patterns in this section, you may choose different options (such as length) than you see in the photos. Once you've created your patterns, the best way to figure out how much yardage to buy is to lay out your pattern pieces on a length of fabric from your stash. Play around with the arrangement so you can buy the least amount of fabric necessary. Snap a photo so you can remember the layout later.

THE BUTTON-UP
button up shirt dress

I love a great shirtdress, and this hack will allow you to make several different looks by changing the length, using the original sleeve, modifying the sleeve into a bishop sleeve (described here), or making it short sleeve. You can make the dress any length you want, and by using different fabrics you can get a variety of looks.

Fabric recommendations: cotton shirting (stripes, plaids, florals) / silks or silky types / lightweight denim or chambray / rayon prints or solids / linen and linen blends

Notions: 10 ½" buttons, 13–15 ½" buttons, lightweight fusible interfacing

Pieces being modified: Button-up *Front, Back, Back Yoke, Sleeve,* and *Front Band*

Pieces needed but not modified: Button-up *Upper Sleeve Placket, Under Sleeve Placket, Upper Collar, Under Collar,* and *Cuff*

FRONT PATTERN PIECE MODIFICATIONS
STEP 1
Trace the FRONT pattern piece on new paper and transfer the dart, center front notch, sleeve notch, and waistline markings (A).

A

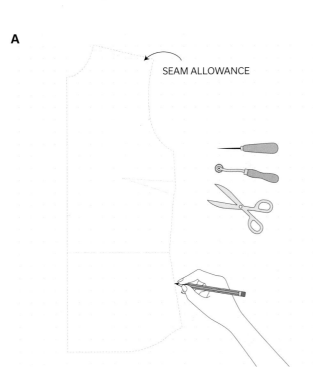

SEAM ALLOWANCE

STEP 2
At the center front, measure down 29" (73.7 cm) from marked waistline and make a hashmark. This measurement is just a guide; you can measure, on your body, from your waist to where you would like the hem of the dress to fall and mark that measurement instead. Once you mark this length, draw a horizontal line at a 90-degree angle from the vertical line across the bottom toward the side seam.

STEP 3

Using a clear ruler, draw a line from the hip at the side seam straight down to the new hemline.

STEP 4

Draw a hashmark about 1″ (2.5 cm) long that is 6″ (15.2 cm) out from the end of the hemline at the side seam. This extra width will add the fullness we want for the shirtdress.

STEP 5

With your measuring tape, measure along the side seam from waist to the hem. The measurement will be slightly more than the first vertical measurement (29″/73.7 cm) because of the fullness of the hip. This is correct, so be sure to use this measurement in step 6.

STEP 6

Extend your measuring tape down from the waistline using the measurement from step 5. This will meet the hashmark you drew in step 4. Now draw a straight line using your yard stick. Draw a mark at that measurement where your tape meets your vertical line.

B (STEPS 2 - 10)

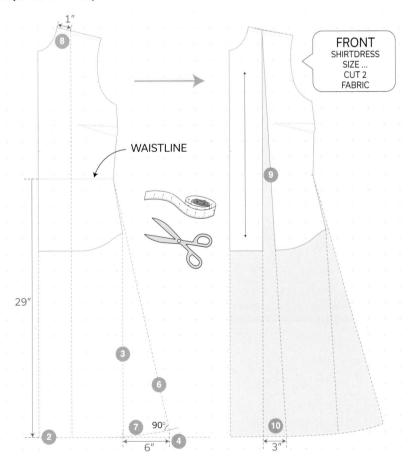

STEP 7

Using your clear ruler, draw a short line at the new hemline/side seam to create a 90-degree angle. Then, using a curved ruler or freehand, you will blend that line to the hemline.

STEP 8

At the shoulder seam nearest the neckline, measure in 1″ (2.5 cm) on the shoulder and draw a straight line down, making sure you are squaring off (perpendicular) to the waistline. Now continue that straight line to the hemline.

- Note: Cut out the pattern pieces at this point so we can slash and spread.

STEP 9

Starting at the hemline, cut along the vertical line you just drew until you almost reach the shoulder and stop. Cut to but not through the seamline, leaving a hinge.

STEP 10

Place a scrap piece of paper long enough to accommodate the length of the dress under the slash and tape down one cut edge. From the taped edge at the hem, spread the slash 3″ (7.6 cm) and tape the other edge, making sure there is no bunching or pulling on the pattern piece. Connect the hemline across the space you have created. Trim off any paper extending beyond the hemline.

- Label your new shirtdress front pattern piece with the following: Front/Shirtdress/Size/Cut 2

BACK PATTERN PIECE MODIFICATIONS

STEP 1

On the yoke pattern piece, mark the ⅜″ (1 cm) seam allowance where it joins the shirt back, and mark the same seam allowance on the shirt back piece (C, D).

C

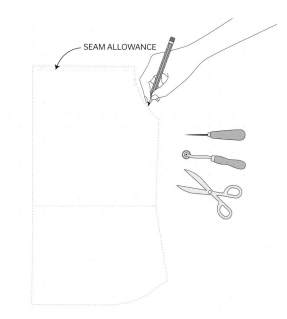

SEAM ALLOWANCE

D

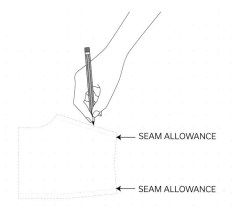

SEAM ALLOWANCE

SEAM ALLOWANCE

STEP 2

Now overlay the yoke on the back so the seam allowance lines you drew overlap one another. Pin in place or tape it down so it doesn't shift; we'll temporarily use the yoke as a guide to add the width to the back as we did to the front, but it will stay a separate pattern piece. Trace the BACK piece on new paper and transfer the back pleat marking, sleeve notches, and waistline marking. Measure down 29" (73.7 cm) from the marked waistline at the center back and draw a vertical line. Once you mark the length, draw a horizontal line at a 90-degree angle from the vertical line across the bottom toward the side seam.

STEP 3

Using the same method as for the front, at the shoulder seam along the neckline measure in 1" (2.5 cm) and draw a straight line down, making sure you are squaring off at the waistline. You can remove the yoke after you have completed this step.

- Follow the instructions for the Front Pattern Piece Modifications, steps 4 through 7, skipping step 8, and finishing with 9 and 10.
- Label your new shirtdress back pattern piece with the following: Back/Shirtdress/Size/Cut 1 on Fold
- Draw your "place on fold" line along the center back.

E (STEPS 2 & 3)

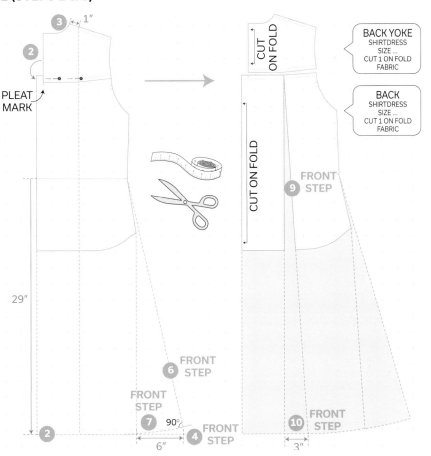

BISHOP SLEEVE MODIFICATION

If you prefer a short sleeve for your shirtdress, skip this sleeve modification and instead follow the instructions for a short sleeve on page 80.

STEP 1

Trace the SLEEVE on new paper and transfer the sleeve notches and placket lines (F).

STEP 2

Fold your sleeve pattern in half vertically, then fold once more in half, then again. These foldlines are now your slash lines. Draw in a line at each fold from the bottom to top and then slash to the top seam allowance but not all the way through, leaving a hinge.

STEP 3

On another piece of paper wide enough to accommodate the spread, mark a straight line down the middle of the paper to mark the grainline. This line is now the center of the sleeve; match the center slash on the sleeve to the grainline on the paper. You should have four slashed pieces on each half of the sleeve. We are going to spread each slash 1" (2.5 cm), so place the two middle slashes ½" (1.3 cm) away from the grainline and tape in place. Continue to spread each slash 1" (2.5 cm) apart and tape them down. Draw a curved line connecting each slash at the hem of the sleeve.

STEP 4

You are going to add length to the sleeve to create the blouson for the bishop sleeve. Using your ruler, draw another line 1" (2.5 cm) below the original hem, following the same curve.

F

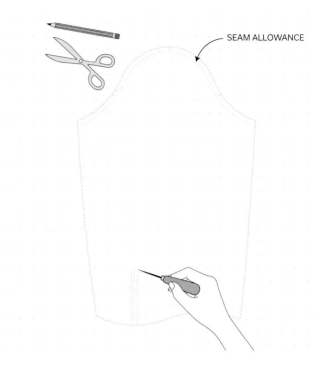

SEAM ALLOWANCE

G (STEPS 2 - 5)

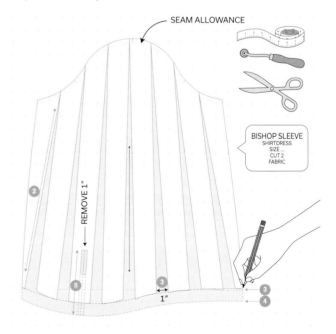

SEAM ALLOWANCE

BISHOP SLEEVE
SHIRTDRESS
SIZE ...
CUT 2
FABRIC

REMOVE 1"

1"

STEP 5

You will need to adjust the placket placement lines on the sleeve pattern by extending the legs to the new hemline. Now remove 1" (2.5 cm) from the top of the placket placement lines. The sleeve placket's length does not change, it just shifts down to the new hem.

- Label your new sleeve pattern piece with the following: Bishop Sleeve/Shirtdress/Size/Cut 2

FRONT BAND MODIFICATION

STEP 1

Trace the FRONT BAND onto new paper, long enough to accommodate the shirtdress length, and transfer the notch. You need to mark the waistline on the front band, and to do that you will need to grab your base pattern front and, making sure the band and shirt are matching up at the hem and at the notch, follow the waistline marking on the front bodice to the band and mark (H).

STEP 2

From the waistline marking you transferred to your band, measure down 29" (73.7 cm). Now extend the band by drawing new lines to match the new length. Make sure you keep the same width all the way down (I). Label your new front band pattern piece with the following:

- Front Band/Shirtdress/Size/Cut 2 Fabric and Interfacing
- If you want to make a belt, measure the circumference of your waist, then multiply that measurement by two. Draw a rectangle that long by 4" (10.2 cm) wide. For belt loops, use the belt loops from the trouser pattern and stitch them to the side seams at the waist of the shirtdress.

SEWING INSTRUCTION

Use the same instructions for the Button-up Shirt (page 37). If you drafted the bishop sleeve, you will need to gather the sleeve hem to fit the cuff versus making the pleats. If you prefer a short sleeve, measure down from your shoulder to your bicep, transfer that measurement to your sleeve pattern and draw a line. Add seam allowance.

H

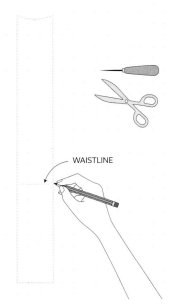

WAISTLINE

I

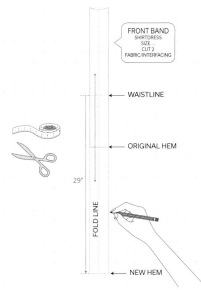

FRONT BAND
SHIRTDRESS
SIZE ___
CUT 2
FABRIC/INTERFACING

WAISTLINE

ORIGINAL HEM

29"

FOLD LINE

NEW HEM

empire button-up shirt with ruffle

This modification is one of my favorites. It's flattering, easy to wear, and you can make it into a dress by simply changing the length. We're also using the under collar piece to change up the look a little too.

Here are few ideas:

- Change the length of the Button-Up shirt to make this a dress, with the ruffle falling at the knee or just above.
- Make the ruffle any width you want to create a different look.
- You can use the short sleeve detailed here, the base pattern's classic sleeve, or the bishop sleeve we created for the shirtdress. Remember that the modifications did not alter the armscye, allowing you to use the sleeves interchangeably.
- Omit the collar completely and finish the neckline with bias tape instead.
- Make the Button-Up shirt's length even shorter and create a cropped shirt with ruffle.

Fabric recommendations: cotton shirting (stripes, plaids, florals) / silks or silky types / lightweight denim or chambray / rayon prints or solids / linen and linen blends

Notions: 6–8 ½" buttons, lightweight interfacing

Pieces being modified: Button-up *Front, Back,* and *Sleeve*

Pieces needed but not modified: *Back Yoke, Under Collar, Front Band,* and *Sleeve Cuff*

FRONT AND BACK BODICE MODIFICATIONS

STEP 1

On your FRONT and BACK bodice base pattern pieces, draw a horizontal line 2" (5 cm) above the waistline (A, B).

A

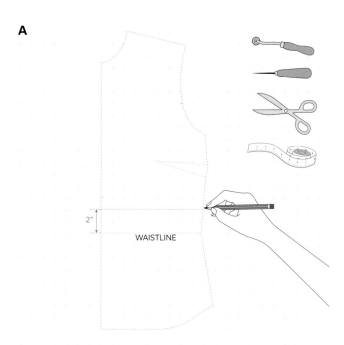

2"

WAISTLINE

B

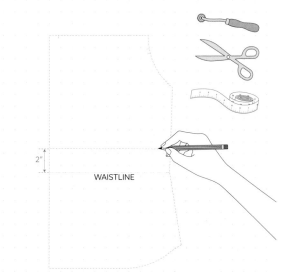

2"

WAISTLINE

STEP 2

Trace your bodice front onto new paper, ending at the new line 2" (5 cm) above the waistline. Transfer the dart and notches on the front. Add a ⅜" (1 cm) seam allowance to the bottom of the front bodice (C).

- Label your new front bodice pattern piece with the following: Front/Empire Button-Up Shirt/Size/Cut 2.

STEP 3

Trace onto new paper the lower part of each of your bodice front and back from the new 2" (5 cm) line above the waistline down. These will become the ruffle pieces. Don't add a seam allowance yet (D).

BACK TOP BODICE MODIFICATION

Trace your bodice back onto new paper, ending at the new line 2" (5 cm) above the waistline. Transfer the notches and pleat line; however, remove the pleat from the new back bodice piece. Align your ruler to the pleat line and draw a straight line down to the bottom of the new bodice. This is the new center back line. Add a ⅜" (1 cm) seam allowance to the bottom of the back bodice (E).

- Label your new back bodice pattern piece with the following: Back/Empire Button-Up Shirt/Size/Cut 1 on fold.
- Draw the "place on fold" line along the Center Back.

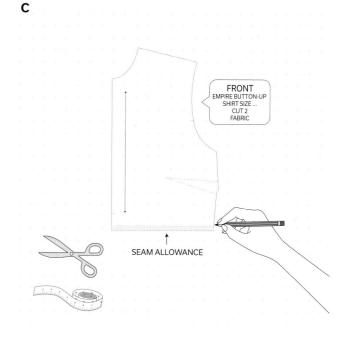

C

FRONT
EMPIRE BUTTON-UP
SHIRT SIZE …
CUT 2
FABRIC

SEAM ALLOWANCE

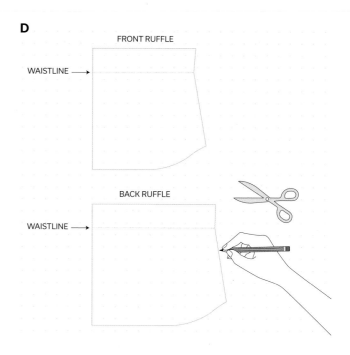

D

FRONT RUFFLE

WAISTLINE →

BACK RUFFLE

WAISTLINE →

E

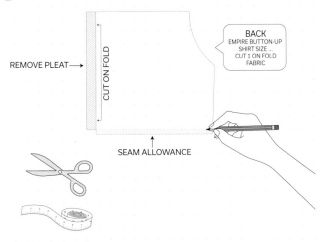

F (STEPS 1 - 3)

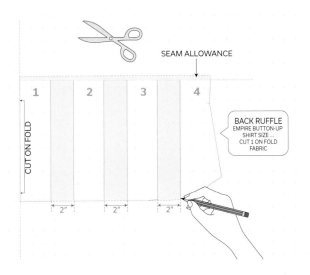

BACK LOWER BODICE MODIFICATION (RUFFLE)

STEP 1

Using the traced bodice back lower half, draw the "place on fold" line along the center back. Now fold the pattern piece in half, matching the upper straight edges of the pattern, then fold in half once again. Draw in the slash lines following the folds. Number each section, then slash along the lines, cutting all the way through each section.

STEP 2

On a new piece of paper, draw a straight vertical guideline and a 90-degree line intersecting it at the top. Place piece #1 along the vertical guideline and top line, then measure 2" (5 cm) from its slashed edge. Draw a line at this mark and tape in place piece #2. Continue until you have spread and taped the remaining pieces. Connect the spaces by drawing a line along the bottom.

STEP 3

Add a seam allowance to the top of this ruffle: measure up ⅜" (1 cm) from the top edge and draw in the seam allowance line. Add the foldline to the center back.

STEP 4

Cut out the new back ruffle pattern piece.

- Label your new lower back bodice pattern piece with the following: Back Ruffle/Empire Button-Up Shirt/Size/Cut 1 on fold

FRONT LOWER BODICE MODIFICATION (RUFFLE)

Fold, slash, and spread the bodice front lower half the same way you did for the back lower half. Be sure to cut the piece on the straight grain, not the fold.

- Label your new lower front bodice pattern piece with the following: Front Ruffle/Empire Button-Up Shirt/Size/Cut 2.

SHORT SLEEVE MODIFICATION

STEP 1

On the base SLEEVE pattern, draw a line across
the sleeve from underarm point to underarm point.
Measure down 4" (10.2 cm) from that line and draw
another horizontal line (G).

STEP 2

Add a 1¼" (3 cm) hem allowance to the bottom of
the sleeve. Draw in your line.

STEP 3

Trace off the sleeve with the new short sleeve hem.
Transfer the notches and grainline.

STEP 4

Fold up your hemline on the paper and then cut to
match the angle of the underarm seam. This will give
the flare needed when sewing the hem (H).

- Label your new shirt sleeve pattern piece with the
  following: Short Sleeve/Empire Button-Up Shirt/
  Size/Cut 2

SEWING INSTRUCTIONS

Follow the Button-Up Shirt instructions (page 37),
but remember that the back pleat has been removed.
Follow along until you get to the hem in Step 6, ignoring
the placket and cuff if you are using the short sleeve
modification—but remember that this is your wardrobe
and you can choose to use the original sleeve with
placket and cuff or the bishop sleeve from the shirt
dress. Sew the side seams of the ruffle together, gather,
and pin to the bottom of the bodice. Stitch using the
⅜" (1 cm) seam allowance and finish the hem of the
ruffle. Then continue with step 7 and add the UNDER
COLLAR only in steps 8 through 10. Make the button-
holes and sew on your buttons to finish.

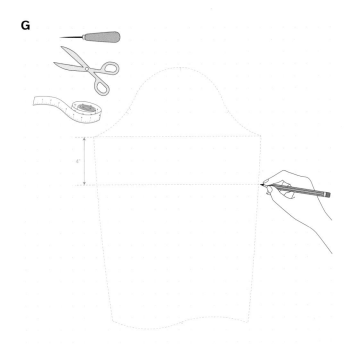

G

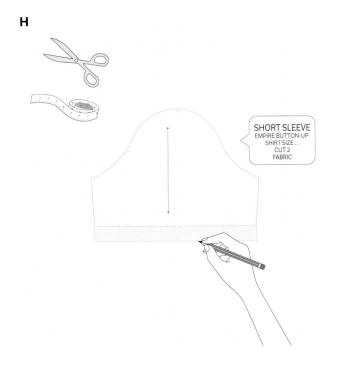

H

SHORT SLEEVE
EMPIRE BUTTON-UP
SHIRT SIZE ...
CUT 2
FABRIC

the shacket

I am obsessed with Shackets (shirt/jackets)! They are fashionable, chic, and can be made from so many fabrics to change the look. As you will see in the final inspiration looks, this one shacket is shown and styled very differently. Make it your own by changing the length and using a variety of fabrics.

Fabric recommendations: flannel (stripes, plaids) / silks or silky types / denim / corduroy / wool and wool blends / boucle / tweeds

Notions: 12–14 ⅝" buttons or snaps, lightweight interfacing

Pieces being modified: Button-up *Front, Back, Sleeve, Back Yoke, Front Band* (or use the one from the shirt-dress for length), *Sleeve Cuff*

Pieces needed but not modified: Button-up *Upper Collar, Under Collar, Placket pieces*

Prep: On the SLEEVE pattern, draw a line from underarm to underarm; this is going to be the bicep line. Then, fold the sleeve in half vertically, so the underarms meet.

FRONT MODIFICATION

STEP 1

Onto new paper, draw a vertical line that is the same length you used for the shirtdress. (You can also choose to make the jacket shorter or longer.) Trace the shirt FRONT onto this paper, placing the pattern's center front on the vertical line. Transfer the waistline marking and notch for the front band (A).

A

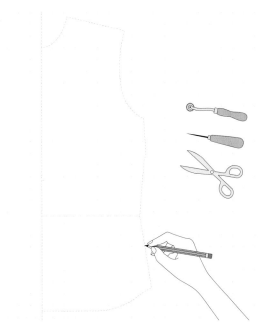

STEP 2

To draft the dropped shoulder, place your ruler on the front's shoulder line and extend the line at least 8" to 10" (20.3 to 25.4 cm) (A). We also need to extend the center front line (B) and then draw a line perpendicular to it that meets the neck/shoulder point (C). Extend line (C) as far as line (A). (See illustration on page 87.)

STEP 3

Using the folded sleeve that has the bicep line drawn on, place it so that the folded edge sits on the extended shoulder line (A) and the top of the sleeve cap touches the shirt front's shoulder. Mark the bicep line on the extended shoulder line.

STEP 4

Draw a line from the bicep marking on the shoulder line up to meet the new top guideline. Now draw a new vertical line from the top guideline at the bicep marking all the way down to the hem; make sure the line is parallel to the center line and that it is the same distance away all the way down the length of the new line.

STEP 5

To accommodate the dropped shoulder, we will be dropping our underarm. From the bicep line at the underarm point, measure down along the new vertical line 11" (27.9 cm) and make a mark. This is the bottom of the new sleeve opening.

STEP 6

Placing your ruler at the widest part of the front bodice at the hem, measure out 1" (2.5 cm) and mark. To create the new side seam, draw a vertical line from this mark up to the level of the sleeve opening mark you made in step 5. Draw a horizontal line from the sleeve opening mark to meet the new side seam you just drew.

STEP 7

Measure down the side seam 2" (5 cm) from the new underarm and mark. Using your French curve ruler, draw a curve from this mark to the sleeve opening (7a).

- Note: If using the same length as the shirtdress, measure down from the waistline 29" (73.7 cm) and square off your hem. (7b)

B (STEPS 2 & 3)

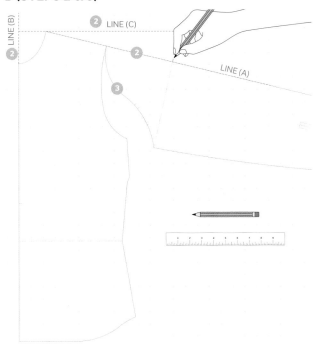

C (STEPS 4 - 7)

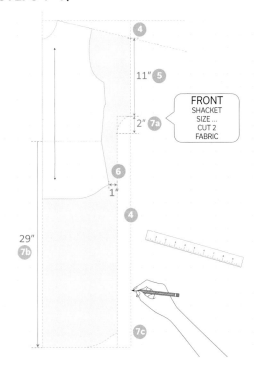

- If you'd like to add a curve to the hem, use the base front pattern and, aligning the hemlines with the side seam point touching the new side seam, transfer the shape of the curve. (7c)

FRONT PATCH POCKETS

STEP 1

Begin drawing your pocket 5″ (12.7 cm) down from the shoulder and 3″ (7.6 cm) in from center front. Draw the pocket onto the shacket front pattern and trace it onto new paper after you are done. A good standard size for the front pocket is 5″ wide × 6″ high (12.7 cm × 15.2 cm), but remember that this is all about you! If you want a bigger pocket, then draw it bigger. I am a fan of streetwear, so I would go for a larger pocket that will make more of a statement.

STEP 2

If you'd like a flap, as I added to a few of the Shacket variations, here's what to do: On scrap paper, draw a box for the pocket flap. Draft the flap the same width as your pocket × 2″ (5 cm) high. You can make the flap taller if your pocket is taller. If you would like a flap with a point, simply measure down ½″ (1.3 cm) from the center of the flap and angle the lines. Add a seam allowance of ½″ (1.3 cm) all the way around the flap.

STEP 3

Place scrap paper under your shacket pattern, and with your tracing wheel, mark your pocket, draw in the lines, and add a seam allowance of ½″ (1.3 cm) at the sides and bottom and a 1″ (2.5 cm) seam allowance at the top of your pocket. NOTE: You will make one final alteration to the front after Step 3 of the Back Modifications, so keep that in mind.

- Cut your new front shacket pattern out. Label the pattern piece with the following: Front/Shacket/Size/Cut 2

D (STEPS 1 - 3)

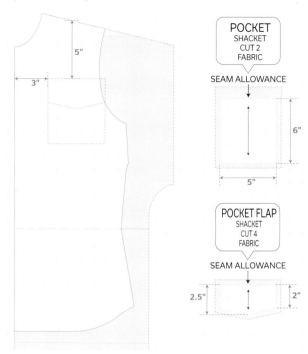

E

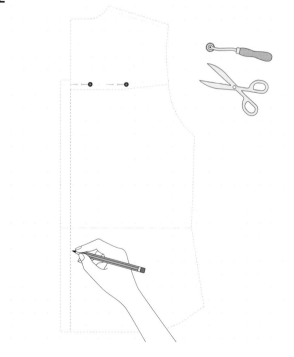

BACK MODIFICATION

Prep: Mark your ⅜″ (1 cm) seam allowance on the BACK YOKE and mark the same seam allowance on the shirt BACK pattern. Align the center back of the yoke pattern to the pleat line on the shirt back matching the seam allowance lines (which is the stitching line). The pleat will extend beyond the yoke; mark the stitching line on the pleat. Pin in place. Following the pleat line on the back piece, draw a straight line from the yoke's neckline all the way down to the shirt back's hem (E).

STEP 1

Draw a long vertical guideline onto new paper to get started. Now draw in another vertical line ¾″ (2 cm) away from the first vertical guideline; this is the distance the pleat extends beyond the yoke. Align the foldlines of the back and yoke pieces (yoke still pinned in place) to the two lines you just drew, as in the diagram. Trace the neckline, shoulder, side seams, and hem. Transfer the waistline marking and mark it all the way across. Use a needle wheel to transfer the stitching line you marked on the pleat to the new paper, remove the pattern, and draw a horizontal line across to the armhole. This is the new yoke line; make sure it is perpendicular to the vertical center foldline.

STEP 2

Place the fully traced front shacket pattern on top of the traced back pattern and align the waistline and neck point. The front pattern now has a higher shoulder than the back, so trace the top of the neck and the shoulder line of the front onto the back. Trace the arm opening, side seam, and hem, making sure the hem extends to the center foldline.

F (STEPS 1 & 2)

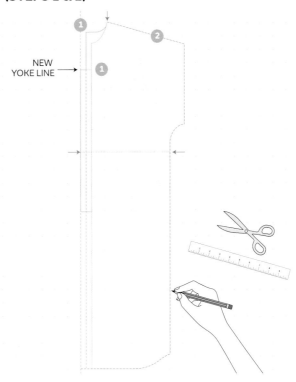

NEW
YOKE LINE →

STEP 3

Because the added height of the shoulder on the back pattern changes the neckline, we now to have make adjustments to the seamlines (called "truing") so the collar will fit. Measuring at the neckline edge, the distance from the original shoulder to the new one you just drew in should be ½" (1.3 cm). This difference will be split between the front and back. Make a mark that is ¼" (6 mm) below the existing shoulder line. Now draw a line below and parallel to the entire shoulder line based on this mark. This is the new cutting line for the back. To true this and make the front and back match, you will also need to cut away ¼" (6 mm) from the front shoulder. These final adjustments will create an armhole opening that is 10¾" (27 cm).

STEP 4

Before cutting out the pattern, you must extend the yoke line to the sleeve opening. Now cut out your yoke from the rest of the pattern. Draw in the foldline along the center back. Cut the rest of your shacket back pattern out.

- You now have two pieces for the back: the yoke and the back. Tape a bit of scrap paper to the bottom of the yoke and the top of the back and draw in a ⅜" (1 cm) seam allowance on each. Mark in the pleat notch.
- Label the pattern piece with the following:
    - Back Yoke/Shacket/Size/Cut 1 on Fold
    - Back/Shacket/Size/Cut 1 on Fold

G (STEPS 3 & 4)

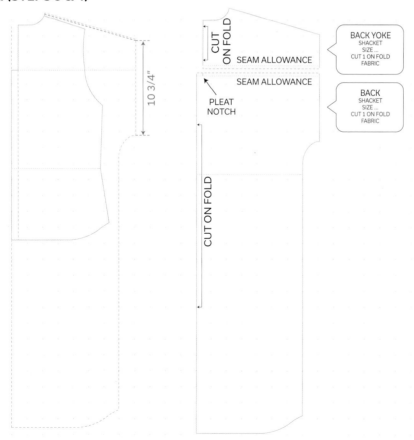

SLEEVE AND CUFF MODIFICATION

STEP 1

Draw a vertical line on new paper and then make a mark about 4" (10.2 cm) below the top of the vertical line. Draw a horizontal line at the mark, extending about 12" in each direction. You are creating a big "T".

STEP 2

Measure out from the vertical line on each side 10¾" (27.3 cm) (this is the armhole measurement from step 3 of the Back Modification) and make a mark on either side.

STEP 3

Open the SLEEVE pattern and place it on your paper so that the center crease is on the vertical line and the bicep line is on the horizontal line. Now we will add a bit of width to the sleeve at the hem. Measure out on either side of the sleeve hem ½" (1.3 cm) and make new marks. Transfer the pleat lines on the sleeve and transfer the placket placement lines.

H (STEPS 1 - 3)

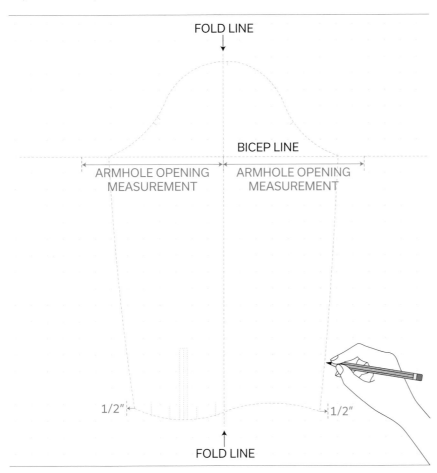

FOLD LINE

BICEP LINE

ARMHOLE OPENING MEASUREMENT   ARMHOLE OPENING MEASUREMENT

1/2"   1/2"

FOLD LINE

STEP 4

Remove the sleeve base pattern and on the new drafted sleeve, draw a line connecting the end of the horizontal line (original bicep line) to the wider sleeve hem markings, extending the curve of the sleeve. Now add ⅜" (1 cm) to the top of the sleeve. Because of the dropped shoulder, we do not use the sleeve cap, hence the new shape of the sleeve. Draw in two notch lines for the sleeve back (the side the placket is on) and one notch on the other side. Cut your sleeve pattern (I).

- Since we added 1" (2.5 cm) to the width of the sleeve at the hem, we need to add that inch to the cuff. Trace out the CUFF onto new paper, measure out 1" (2.5 cm) from one short end, extending the top and bottom cuff edges, and draw a vertical line. Draw in the foldline. Cut your cuff pattern (J).
- Label the pattern piece with the following: Sleeve Cuff/Shacket/Cut 2 Fabric, Cut 2 Interfacing.

SEWING INSTRUCTIONS

The Button-Up shirt base pattern instructions apply for the collar band, front band, sleeve, placket, and hem. Finish the edges of the patch pockets and hem the top edges, then pin them in place before you sew them to the front; I like to make sure I like the placement before stitching them down. Attach the shacket front to the back at the shoulders. When you're happy with the placement, sew on the pocket. If you cut flaps, two will be the flaps and two will be the facings. Put one of each RS together, stitch, turn, and press; repeat for the other flap. Then with the raw edge of the pocket flap ⅜" (1 cm) from the top of the pocket and pointing away from the pocket, stitch the flap to the shirt. Now fold down the pocket flap and topstitch.

Because this has a dropped shoulder, the sleeve is easier to insert, match your shoulder seam, pin, and stitch. Then sew up the underarm seam and side seam in one continuous seam. Continue the same as for the base pattern for the cuff.

I

SEAM ALLOWANCE

SLEEVE
SHACKET
SIZE ...
CUT 2
FABRIC

J

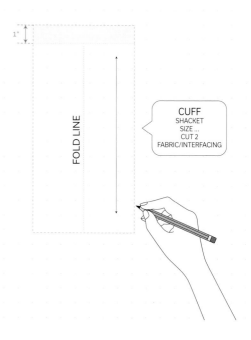

1"

FOLD LINE

CUFF
SHACKET
SIZE ...
CUT 2
FABRIC/INTERFACING

THE TROUSER
drop crotch pants

Ok, I know drop crotch pants are not for everyone, but remember that this only means the crotch is dropped lower than your average trouser/pant. It doesn't mean you need to drop it as much as I would. By simply dropping the crotch a few inches you will get a relaxed pleated pant that works great for so many looks.

Fabric recommendations: rayon prints or solids / silks or silky types / lightweight denim or chambray / linen and linen blends / twills

Notions: 1 ¾" button, 9" zipper, lightweight interfacing

Pieces being modified: Trouser *Front, Back*

Pieces needed but not modified: Trouser *Waistband, Pocket pieces*

PREP
STEP 1
Measure and mark a line that is 1" (2.5 cm) in from the FRONT fly extension.

STEP 2
(Optional) Fold up the BACK and FRONT trouser leg so the hem meets the knee marking. That new foldline will be the new length (A, B).

A

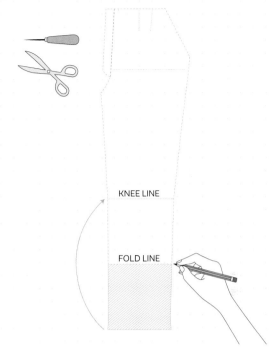

B

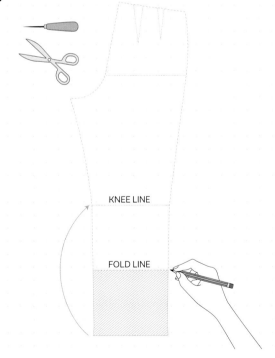

BACK PANT PATTERN MODIFICATION

STEP 1

Starting with our BACK trouser piece: Draw a straight line on new paper and line up the straightest part of the center back, or back crotch seam, of the trouser pattern on your line, and transfer the notches to the line. This will change the grainline, but that is OK. Make sure you give yourself space at the top of the paper. Mark the knee length on the vertical line. Draw a line perpendicular to the vertical line at this mark; this is our knee line.

STEP 2

We are now going to determine the drop of the crotch. I marked 4" (10.2 cm) up from the knee, but this is also optional. You can bring the crotch up more or drop it more.

STEP 3

With the center back of the trouser pattern on the vertical line, trace the waistline from the center back to the end of the first dart. Mark the dart legs and dart point. Place your finger on the top of the dart and swing the pattern until half of the crotch curve is on either side of the vertical line. Now continue tracing the waistline until you get to the end of the second dart.

STEP 4

Holding the second dart in place, swing the pattern until the tip of the crotch is on the vertical line again. Continue tracing the top of the waistband. Trace the outseam from the top of the waistband to the new hem foldline. Trace the inseam from the new hem to the knee line. Mark the dart legs and dart point for the second dart. Trace in both your darts.

C (STEPS 1 - 3)

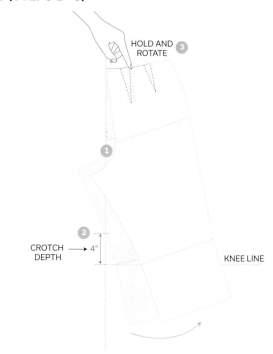

D (STEPS 4 & 5)

STEP 5

Measure the distance from the first vertical line you drew to the knee line. Keep this measurement in mind, as we will use it for the front. I will refer to this is as the drop depth. Now working from the drop crotch marking we measured in step 2 (4" [10.2 cm] up from knee line), mark a short line to create a 90-degree angle and draw a curve from that line to the knee line.

STEP 6

Draw a line to connect your outseam and inseam to create a hemline. Add a grainline by folding vertically so the knee notch and hem on each side are aligned and make a crease. Draw in your line and cut out the pattern piece (E).

FRONT PANT LEG MODIFICATION

STEP 1

Draw a straight line on a new sheet of paper the same as you did for the back. Align the line you drew on the FRONT fly along the vertical line; this is the center front. Trace in the fly front and mark the knee. Draw a guideline across at the knee, making sure it is perpendicular to the vertical guideline. Mark the drop crotch measurement—I used 4" (10.2 cm) for the back, so use the same for the front. Now mark the measurement you noted in step 5 for the Back modifications (drop depth) on your front knee line.

E

BACK
DROP-CROTCH PANTS
SIZE ...
CUT 2
FABRIC

F (STEPS 1 & 2)

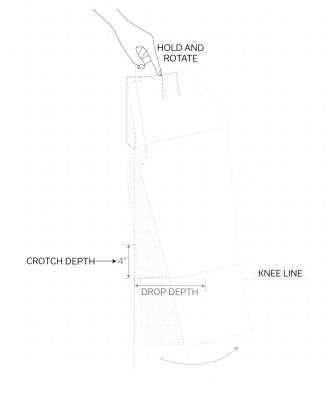

HOLD AND
ROTATE

CROTCH DEPTH ⟶ 4"

DROP DEPTH

KNEE LINE

STEP 2

Align the front pattern to the vertical line again and trace the waist until you reach the first pleat line. Holding your pattern at the pleat, swing the pattern until the inseam is on the halfway point of the drop depth. Continue tracing the waistline until you reach the other pleat line.

STEP 3

Swing the pattern again until the inseam is at the full drop depth marking. Trace the remaining part of the waist and the outseam to the new hem; remember to trace the notches. Trace the inseam to the knee and draw in the curve the same as for the back (G).

STEP 4

Mark in the pleat legs. Draw a line to connect the outseam and inseam to create a hemline. Add a grainline as for the back, step 6 (H).

SEWING INSTRUCTIONS

Use the sewing instructions for the Trousers base pattern (see page 42). The shape of the pant leg has changed, but the order of the construction remains the same. If you choose to add the cuff, press up the entire allowance, stitch, then press up the cuff, and tack at the side seam at the hem if needed.

G

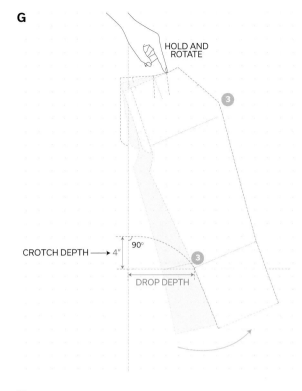

H

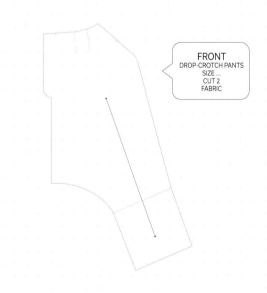

elastic-waist palazzo pants

Who doesn't need a great pair of pull-on palazzo pants that are quick and easy to make and are so flattering? You can make these any length you'd like—maxi-length, midi-length, or even knee-length for a great pair of shorts!

Pieces being modified: Trouser *Front, Back, Waist-band, Pocket Bag*

Fabric recommendations: cotton (stripes, plaids, florals) / silks or silky types / lightweight denim or chambray / rayon prints or solids / linen and linen blends / crepe

Notions: 1½" wide elastic

STEP 1

You will not be using the pocket from the Trouser pattern, so you need to adjust the pattern. Align the waist edge and hip edge of the POCKET BAG on the FRONT trouser leg. Pin the pocket to the front.

STEP 2

Fold back the fly extension; these pants don't need it. Trace the front onto new paper. Mark the hipline and knee line. You do not need to transfer the pleat (A).

STEP 3

Trace the BACK trouser pattern onto new paper. Mark the hipline and knee line. You do not need to transfer the darts (B).

- If you want to make shorts, simply mark the knee line as the new hemline.

A

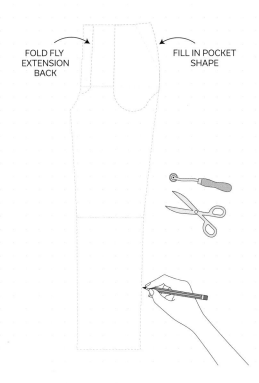

FOLD FLY EXTENSION BACK

FILL IN POCKET SHAPE

B

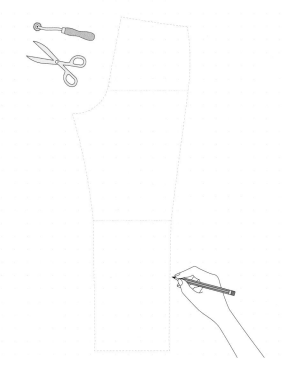

FRONT AND BACK PANT LEG MODIFICATIONS

STEP 1

You will be making very similar modifications to the front and back pieces. First you will square off the outseam, because these pants don't need the leg curve. On the pant back, draw a line extending the hemline a few inches and then draw a straight line from the pant hipline to the extended hemline.

STEP 2

On the back pant piece, measure the distance from the original outseam to the new outseam at the hemline. Use that measurement to extend the front pant leg hem. Then draw a straight line down from the hipline to meet the new extended hemline.

STEP 3

On the front and back inseams, extend the hemline ½" (1.3 cm) and draw a line straight down from the knee line to the new hemline.

STEP 4

Cut out the patterns and fold each in half vertically, matching up the hemlines at the outseams. This is the slash line to add width.

STEP 5

Unfold the patterns. Following the crease, cut all the way through the patterns from hem to waist.
Do the following for both front and back pant legs:
On a new piece of paper, draw a straight vertical line. Align and tape one side of the slashed pant leg to the line. Measure out 4" (10.2 cm) from the line and draw another straight line parallel to it. Tape down the other side of the pant leg to the second line. Mark the hiplines and knee lines on the new pant legs. Draw in the new grainlines, using one taped edge as a guide.

STEP 6

Connect the waistline across the slash and trim off paper above the waist; do the same for the hemline. Mark the ⅜" (1 cm) seam allowance on the front and back crotch, inseams, and outseams, and then measure from seamline to seamline at the waist and note that measurement. Add the back and front measurements for half of the full waist circumference.

ELASTIC WAISTBAND

STEP 1

Using the WAISTBAND as a guide for width, trace its long edges. Draw a vertical line to close one end of the waistband and mark it as center front (E). Use the measurement in step 6 for the length, draw a vertical line to close the remaining end, and add ⅜" (1 cm) seam allowance (F).

- Label your new waistband pattern piece with the following: Waistband/Palazzo Pants/Size/Cut 1 on Fold

SEWING INSTRUCTIONS

Stitch the front RS together at the crotch; repeat for the back. With RS together, sew front to back at the inseams and outseams. Place the waistband's short ends RS together and stitch; you now have a ring. Fold the waistband in half, WS together, and press. Attach the waistband to the waist, placing the seam at the back crotch seam, and stitch using a ⅜" (1 cm) seam allowance. Leave an opening 1" (2.5 cm) in length to insert the elastic. Once the elastic is inserted, stitch the elastic ends together and finish stitching the opening closed. Press the waistband up and stitch the pant hems.

C (BACK, STEPS 1 - 6)

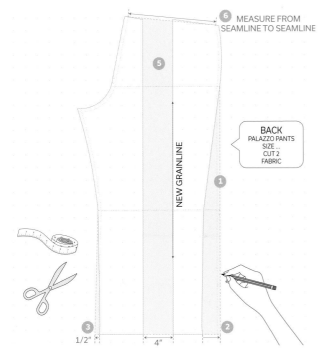

⑥ MEASURE FROM SEAMLINE TO SEAMLINE

⑤

NEW GRAINLINE

BACK
PALAZZO PANTS
SIZE ...
CUT 2
FABRIC

①

③
1/2"

②

4"

E

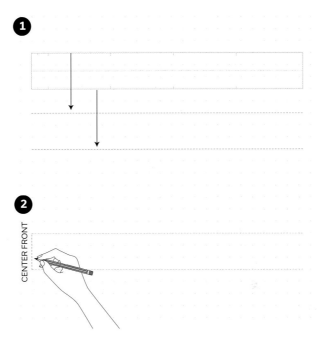

①

② CENTER FRONT

D (FRONT, STEPS 2 - 6)

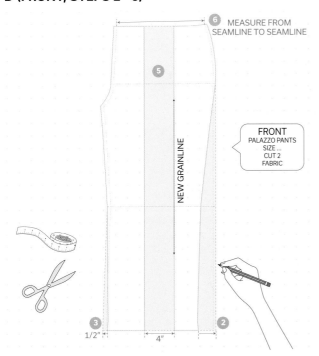

⑥ MEASURE FROM SEAMLINE TO SEAMLINE

⑤

NEW GRAINLINE

FRONT
PALAZZO PANTS
SIZE ...
CUT 2
FABRIC

③
1/2"

②

4"

F

WAISTBAND
PALAZZO PANTS
SIZE ...
CUT 1 ON FOLD
FABRIC/INTERFACING

CENTER FRONT

CUT ON FOLD

SEAM ALLOWANCE →

= (BACK+FRONT)

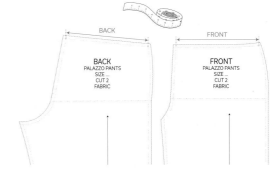

BACK

FRONT

BACK
PALAZZO PANTS
SIZE ...
CUT 2
FABRIC

FRONT
PALAZZO PANTS
SIZE ...
CUT 2
FABRIC

wide-leg pants

The base Trouser pattern has a beautiful high waist, pleated front, and a slim leg, but in this modification, you will turn these slim-leg trousers into wide-leg, flat-front pants. I love a high-waist wide-leg pant, because as a short five-foot, four-inch curvy Latina the high waist and wide leg make me look taller and accentuate my shape. You can make this your own by choosing not to remove the front pleats, by changing the length for a wide-leg cropped look, or by using a variety of fabrics to change the style. A silky fabric will give you a flowing look, whereas a denim or medium-weight twill will give you a stiffer look, much like a pair of jeans—especially if you add contrasting topstitching.

Pieces being modified: Trouser *Front, Back*

Pieces needed but not modified: Trouser *Waistband, Pocket Bag, Pocket Facing, Belt Loops*

Fabric Recommendations: denim / silks or silky types / corduroy / rayon prints or solids / linen and linen blends / twills

Notions: ¾" button, 9" zipper, lightweight interfacing

STEP 1

Trace the trouser FRONT and trouser BACK onto new sheets of paper. Transfer the knee notch, hipline, and back darts. You will be eliminating the pleat in the front, but you'll need to place hashmarks at the waistline for reference (A, B).

A

PLEAT PLACEMENT FOR REFERENCE ONLY

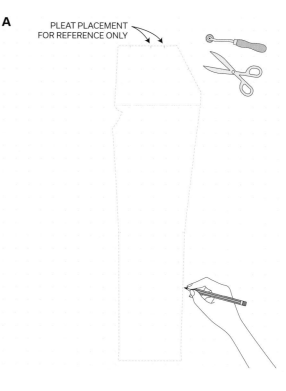

B

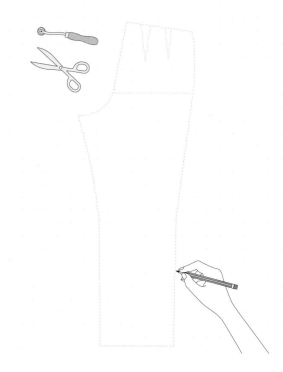

STEP 2

Starting with the front, fold the leg vertically, matching up the pleat lines to find the middle. Crease all the way down, making sure the knee notches and hem are on the same level, even though they won't meet at the side seams. Unfold the pattern.

STEP 3

Mark where the crease falls on the hemline. Draw a straight line from one pleat line to the hemline crease marking and do the same for the other pleat line; this creates a big dart. You need to remove this dart, which eliminates the pleat.

STEP 4

Make a cut from the bottom of the paper just to, but not through, the hemline crease marking. Now cut along the marked pleat/dart line closest to the outseam; cut from the waist edge to the hemline crease marking but not through, creating a hinge (4a). Now bring the cut line to meet the other pleat/dart line, closing it. Tape it in place. Square off the hemline by drawing a line across from the original inseam to original outseam (4b).

C (STEPS 2 - 5)

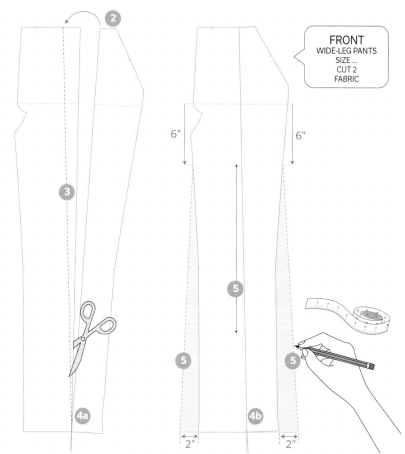

FRONT
WIDE-LEG PANTS
SIZE ...
CUT 2
FABRIC

STEP 5

Measure out 2" (5 cm) on the outseam at the hem and 2" (5 cm) at the inseam to create the wide leg. Measure down 6" (15.2 cm) from the hipline at the outseam and mark. Using your yardstick, draw a line from the new wider hem to the mark 6" (15.2 cm) below the hipline. For the inseam, again using your yardstick, draw a straight line from the wider hem up to the blending point, 6" (15.2 cm) from the hip, and draw a line. Blend each line into its original seamline, using a curved ruler. Fold the pant leg pattern in half, matching the knee notches and hemline at the inseam and outseam. Crease the paper to mark a new grainline and draw it in.

STEP 6

Follow step 5 to make the same the wide-leg adjustment to the back pant pattern (D).

SEWING INSTRUCTIONS

Follow the instructions for the Trousers base pattern. The only difference here is the removal of the front pleat.

D

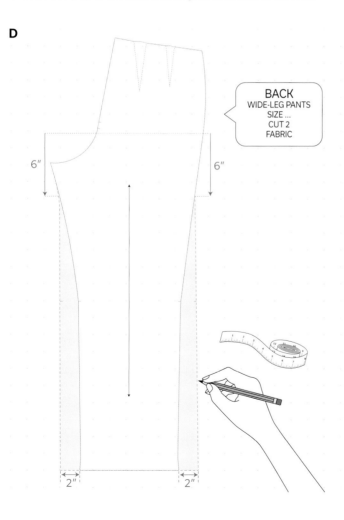

BACK
WIDE-LEG PANTS
SIZE ...
CUT 2
FABRIC

6" 6"

2" 2"

THE PENCIL SKIRT
denim skirt

Everyone needs a denim skirt in their life! Now, that doesn't mean you have to only use denim. You can make this skirt out of any stretch woven fabric. You can also make this skirt midi-length or just below the knee. Add topstitching for a true jeans look.

Pieces being modified: Pencil Skirt *Front,* Pencil Skirt *Waistband,* Trouser *Pocket Bag*

Additional pattern pieces needed: Pencil Skirt *Back,* Trouser *Front,* Trouser *Pocket Facing,*

Fabric recommendations: stretch denim / stretch corduroy / stretch sateen/ double knits

Notions: ⅝" button or snap, 9" zipper, lightweight interfacing

STEP 1

Because you are using some pattern pieces from the pant pattern to create the denim skirt, you need to mark the center front on the Trouser FRONT's fly extension. From the outer edge of the fly, measure in 1" (2.5 cm) and draw a straight line from the waist edge to the bottom of the extension; set aside for use later.

STEP 2

Draw a vertical line on new paper. Trace the skirt FRONT and skirt BACK onto the paper; transfer the notches, darts, and hipline. You will not be altering the skirt back piece, so you can go ahead and cut that out (A).

A

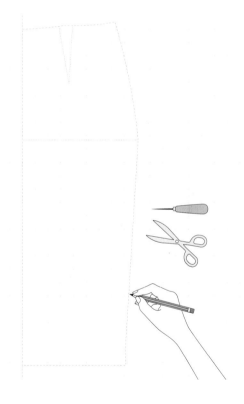

STEP 3

Since the base Pencil Skirt front pattern is cut on the fold, you need to add a ⅜" (1 cm) seam allowance to the center front to accommodate the fly. Place the trouser front on top of the skirt front, making sure the center front marking on the fly extension from step 1 aligns to the new center front seam allowance line. Trace the fly extension onto the paper.

STEP 4

Place the trouser's POCKET BAG pattern onto the skirt front, aligning the top edge with the skirt waistline and the pocket's hip curve along a portion of the skirt's side seam. You will notice the pocket bag sits farther in from the skirt's side seam, so you need to extend the pocket bag. Trace around the pocket directly onto the skirt and extend the pocket's hip curve to meet the side seam. Now, with your tracing wheel and the pocket still in place, trace over the diagonal pocket opening line to mark it on the skirt.

STEP 5

Remove the pocket and, following the markings of the tracing wheel, draw in the pocket opening line on the skirt front, extending it to the side seam. Add a ⅜" (1 cm) seam allowance to the line for the pocket opening. Cut out your pattern.

B (STEPS 3 - 5)

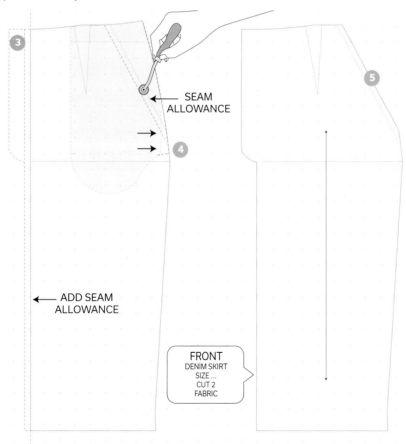

SEAM ALLOWANCE

ADD SEAM ALLOWANCE

FRONT
DENIM SKIRT
SIZE ...
CUT 2
FABRIC

STEP 6

Fold in half another piece of paper that is big enough to accommodate the pocket. Place your folded paper underneath the skirt and trace with your tracing wheel the shape of the pocket bag, the pocket opening line, and the seam allowance at the opening line. Draw in the lines created by your tracing wheel.

STEP 7

Cut out the pocket bag pattern from both layers of paper. You will have two pocket bags since you cut folded paper. Leave one as is; on the other one, cut off along the seam allowance line at the pocket opening. Add a vertical grainline. Now you have a pocket bag and a pocket facing.

C (STEPS 6 & 7)

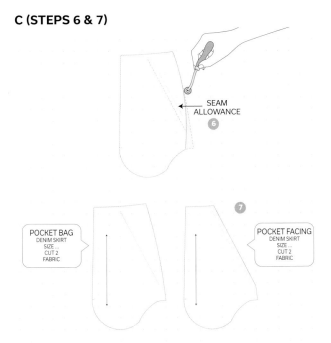

WAISTBAND

Trace the Pencil Skirt WAISTBAND onto new paper. Because you have created a fly front, the waistband needs to open at the center front. Label the center front notches as center back and, while sewing the waistband on, disregard the side seam notches as they will not match up.

- Label your new pattern pieces with the following: Front/Denim Skirt/Size/Cut 2; Back/Denim Skirt/ Size/Cut 2; Waistband/Denim Skirt/Size/Cut 1 main fabric, and 1 interfacing

SEWING INSTRUCTIONS

For this skirt, you will be using the instructions for the base pattern Trousers (page 42) for the fly front, pockets, and waistband. For the skirt's center back, finish the vent following the Pencil Skirt (page 47) instructions. Once you have sewn the fly front and attached the pockets, pin and sew the side seams. Attach the waistband as for the trousers and sew the hem. If you are making this out of denim, pay close attention to your topstitching and use the tips given for sewing with denim in the fabric section (see page 17).

full gathered skirt

This skirt is my most popular tutorial ever! It is the regal maxi skirt, and of course it can be made in various lengths. Fabric choice plays a big part here because it can be made from so many fabrics, and based on what you pick, you will have a skirt that either falls gently around the body or adds volume.

Pieces being modified: Pencil Skirt *Front* and *Back*

Additional pattern pieces needed: Trouser *Pocket Bag*, Pencil Skirt *Waistband*

Fabric recommendations: cottons / scuba knits / lightweight denim / rayon prints or solids / linen / silk or silky types

Notions: lightweight interfacing, 12–14" invisible zipper

Prep: Decide where you want the hem to land; this is a personal choice. If it's longer than the Pencil Skirt base pattern, jot down the length you want and use this measurement in step 1. If you prefer a mini version, you can shorten the pattern to the height of the back vent.

STEP 1

Start with a vertical guideline for each piece. Trace the skirt front and skirt back onto new paper, extending to the new length if necessary. You don't need to mark or transfer the darts, as you will be taking them up in the fullness of the gathered skirt. Transfer the skirt hipline and center back notch; you don't need the vent. Square off the hem at the desired length and draw a new hemline (A, B).

A (FRONT)

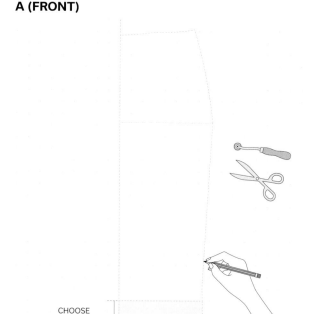

CHOOSE PREFERRED LENGTH

B (BACK)

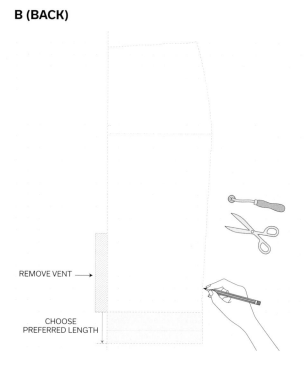

REMOVE VENT →

CHOOSE PREFERRED LENGTH

STEP 2

Because you are using the base Pencil Skirt pattern, you must remove the pegged shape on both the front and back pattern pieces. Extend the hemline several inches to the side to give yourself room. From the hipline down, draw a straight line to the hemline, and square it off.

STEP 3

We are going to add 10" (25.4 cm) to the front and 10" to the back (you can choose to do less if you want fewer gathers and less volume—just choose an even number). To allow you to slash and spread the skirt, create two slash lines from hem to waist. You don't have to be too precise about where they are; figure one-third of the measurement of the waist and space them that distance apart from either side of the waistline. Cut along both lines from top to bottom and number your pieces.

STEP 4

Draw a vertical line on new paper, square off at the bottom, and draw in a horizontal hemline – a big "L". Tape the first slashed skirt piece at its center front or center back to the vertical line. Spread each slash 5" (12.7 cm), making sure the bottom sits on the horizontal hemline you drew. Draw in the hemline and waistline. Repeat for the back skirt piece. Mark the center front with a foldline.

- If you're using a larger size and the skirt front piece doesn't fit onto your folded fabric, you can add a center front seam. Simply add ⅜" (1 cm) to the center front edge and cut 2 skirt fronts instead of cutting 1 on the fold. This will allow you more room and the seam will be lost in the gathers.

C (FRONT, STEPS 2 - 4)

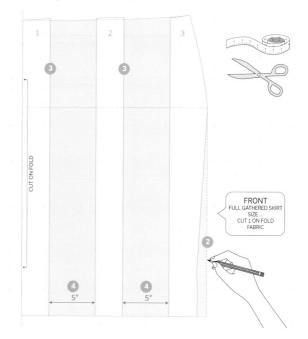

CUT ON FOLD

FRONT
FULL GATHERED SKIRT
SIZE ...
CUT 1 ON FOLD
FABRIC

STEP 5

Cut the new pattern pieces. If you would like to add a side seam pocket, you will use the pocket bag pattern piece from the Trouser pattern. It will need a slight alteration; align it to the skirt front and side seam as closely as possible, then trace the long curved edge onto the skirt front. Remove the pattern piece. Transfer the altered shape (including side and waist) to a new piece of paper by tracing with paper on top, or use a tracing wheel onto paper below. Cut out the new pieces; you'll need to cut four from fabric.

- Label your new pattern pieces with the following: Front/Gathered Skirt/Size/Cut 1 on Fold; Back/Gathered Skirt/Size/Cut 2; Side Seam Pocket/Gathered Skirt/Size/Cut 4

SEWING INSTRUCTIONS

I find it easier to sew gathering rows at the waist of the front and back separately before stitching them together at the side seams. If you are adding side seam pockets, stitch your pockets to the top of the front and back side seams; press the pockets and seam allowances away from the skirt, understitching the pockets. Pin at the side seams and sew from the hem up, stopping 1" (2.5 cm) above the bottom of the pocket;

backstitch and break your thread. Move up to 1" (2.5 cm) below the top of the pocket and backstitch, then sew the rest of the side seam. This creates your pocket opening. Then stitch around the edges of the pocket bag itself. Fold the waistband in half WS together and gather the skirt to fit the waistband. Add a zipper and finish the waistband as in the Pencil Skirt instructions. Press up and sew your hem. If you'd like, add a bow or other adornment to the waist.

D (BACK, STEPS 2 - 4)

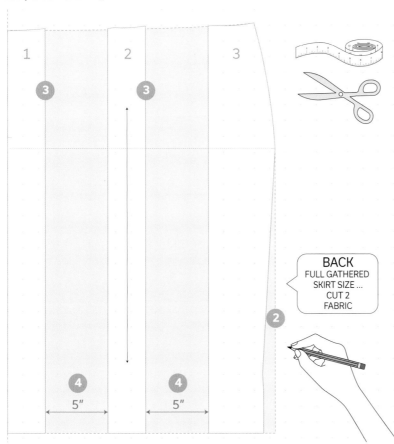

BACK
FULL GATHERED
SKIRT SIZE ...
CUT 2
FABRIC

a-line princess skirt

This is one of my favorite skirts to make and wear! It is an A-line skirt with front slits that are optional but add a lot. It can be made any length you choose and from so many fabrics.

Pieces being modified: Pencil Skirt *Front*, Pencil Skirt *Back*

Additional pattern pieces needed: Trouser *Pocket (optional)*, Pencil Skirt *Waistband*

Fabric recommendations: cotton (stripes, plaids, florals) / silks or silky types / lightweight denim or chambray / rayon prints or solids / linen and linen blends / crepe

Notions: lightweight interfacing, 12–14" invisible zipper

A (BACK, STEPS 1 - 4)

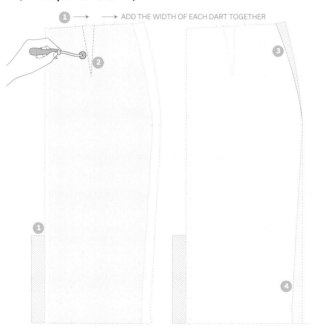

① → → ADD THE WIDTH OF EACH DART TOGETHER

PREP

STEP 1

Trace the skirt FRONT pattern onto new paper, as is. Transfer the dart and notches. Trace the skirt BACK, minus the back vent, and transfer the notches—but only mark the top of the dart legs at the waist with a hashmark, notch, or line. (Instead of using these darts, you'll be transferring the front dart to the skirt back.) Measure the width of each dart that you marked on the back waist and add the numbers together; you'll use this measurement in step 3. Draw in a ⅜" (1 cm) seam allowance along the skirt's center back.

STEP 2

Place the front base pattern piece on top of the traced back skirt pattern and align the center front of the skirt with the new seam allowance line. Now trace the front's full dart onto the back.

STEP 3

Measure the width of the new dart and subtract that number from the measurement you noted in step 1. To compensate for the difference between the size of the darts, you'll need to remove that amount from the skirt back. (As an example, if the back darts measured a total of 2" (5 cm) and the front dart measured 1⅛" (2.8 cm), you'll need to remove ⅞" (2.2 cm) from the skirt back.) Measure in your amount from the back's side seam and mark at the waistline. Now draw a curve from the waist back into the hip, using a French curve or hip curve ruler to blend the line at the side seam.

STEP 4

Because you are using the base Pencil Skirt pattern, you must remove the pegged hem. On the front and back skirt, extend the hemline several inches to give yourself room. Then from the hipline down, draw a straight line to the hemline, and square it off. Complete the hemline.

FRONT MODIFICATIONS

STEP 1

Cut out the front skirt pattern.

STEP 2

Draw a straight line from the tip of the dart to the hem. Measure the distance from the center front to the dart point. You will use this measurement to make sure you are drawing a straight line parallel to the center front. Several inches down from the dart point, measure that distance from the center front and mark a dash; do this until you reach the hem. Now connect the dashes to create one complete vertical line.

STEP 3

Now let's cut and create a hinge. Starting at the hem, cut along the drawn line up to the dart point but not through it. Then, from the waist, cut along the dart leg closest to the center front to the point but not through it, so that the dart point becomes the hinge.

STEP 4

Swing the pattern open at the hem, bringing the cut dart leg to meet the other dart leg. Tape it down. This creates the A-line flare. Using scrap paper, fill in the space and tape it down. Blend the lines to connect the flare at the hem.

B (FRONT, STEP 4)

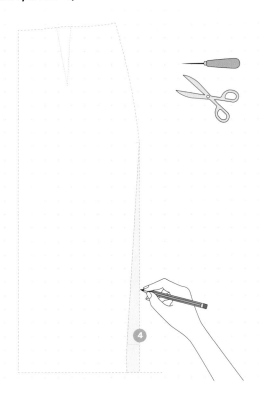

STEP 5

Tape scrap paper to the side seam to add more width. Measure the distance between the cut lines at the hem; take half of that measurement and make a mark at the side seam so you can extend the hemline. Now, measure up along the existing side seam to the hipline and note the measurement. (You need this measurement to properly add the width to the skirt at the side.) Following the angle of the hip, use the ruler to mark the amount you just measured. Draw in the new side seam line down to the hem, where the marks meet. Mark a short 90-degree line and, using a curved ruler, blend into the existing hemline. Cut away the excess paper.

STEP 6

Let's create the princess seams. Find the halfway point of the distance between the cut lines on the skirt front. Draw a straight line up to the dart point. Now cut all the way up, following the line. Your skirt front is now two pieces. Using scrap paper, tape down the cut edges and draw in a ⅜" (1 cm) seam allowance for both pieces. Add a notch about 6" (15.2 cm) or so below the hip if you want to add slits. To find the grainline for the side front, fold in half so the piece is aligned at the hem, crease, and draw a line. (It won't exactly match at the waist, which is okay.) (D)

- Label the new pattern pieces with the following: Center Front/A-line Skirt/Cut 1 on Fold; Side Front/A-line Skirt/Cut 2

D

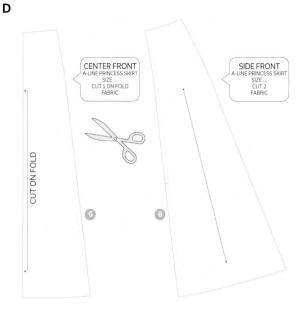

C (STEPS 2 - 6)

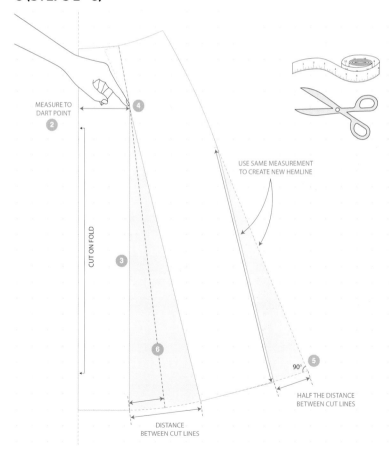

BACK MODIFICATIONS

STEP 1

Follow the same steps given for the front from step 2 through 6. (E) It may be helpful to add a set of double notches along the princess seam in the back pieces to distinguish them from the front (F).

- Note: The only thing you must make sure of is that the measurement from step 4 is also used on the back. If it is not the same, swing the dart closed a bit more or overlap it less to get the same measurement as for the front.

- Label the half that has the original seam Center Back/A-line Skirt/Cut 2; label the other piece Side Back/A-line Skirt/Cut 2

SEWING INSTRUCTIONS

Start by stitching the center front to the side front and deciding if you want the hem slits or not. If not, simply sew the entire seam from waist to hem. If you want the slits, sew the seams from the waist to the mark added in step 6 (or it can be any number of inches above the hem you wish) and press the seam allowances open so you can stitch the seam allowance on each side. Do the same for the skirt back: stitch the center back to the side back. Stitch the center back seam from the hem up to the back notch. Install the zipper of your choice. Now sew your side seams together. Finish the skirt waistband the same as the Pencil Skirt (see page 47). Press and stitch the hem.

E

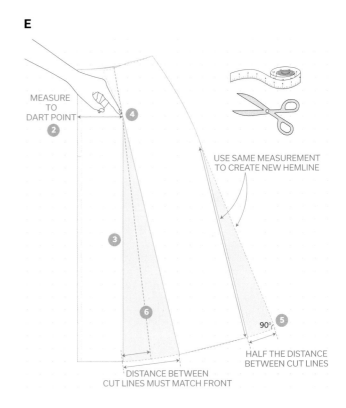

MEASURE TO DART POINT

USE SAME MEASUREMENT TO CREATE NEW HEMLINE

90°

HALF THE DISTANCE BETWEEN CUT LINES

DISTANCE BETWEEN CUT LINES MUST MATCH FRONT

F

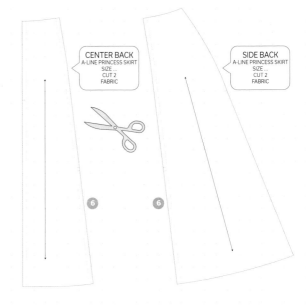

CENTER BACK A-LINE PRINCESS SKIRT SIZE ... CUT 2 FABRIC

SIDE BACK A-LINE PRINCESS SKIRT SIZE ... CUT 2 FABRIC

THE FITTED TEE
dropped waist t-shirt dress

I love outfits that are cute and comfy to wear and this dress hits both marks. It is so cute! I love the shape and the knit fabric options you have for this cute little number. You can choose to make this a mini or knee-length, decide how deep you want the ruffle, and even choose a U-neck or V-neck.

Pieces being modified: Fitted Tee *Front, Back,* and *Sleeve*

Additional pattern pieces needed: Fitted Tee *Neckband*

Fabric recommendations: jersey knits / cotton knits / ribbed knits (for cuff and/or for dress) / French terry / sweatshirt fleece

PREP

STEP 1

Trace the FRONT, BACK, and SLEEVE onto new paper. Transfer all notches (A).

A

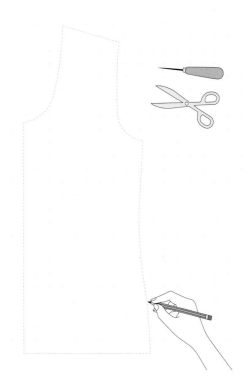

STEP 2

Draw in slash lines on the front and back pieces; you do not want to slash at the neckline, so mark the first slash line on the inner shoulder ½" (1.3 cm) from the neck, and mark another slash line ¾" (1.9 cm) away from the outer shoulder. Draw the third slash line 1½" (3.8 cm) from the underarm.

FRONT AND BACK

STEP 1

Starting with the front, cut the slash lines from the hem up to the top but not through the seamline, creating a hinge. Place the slashed pattern on top of scrap paper so you can spread the pattern and tape it down. Place a weight at the top neck to keep the pattern from shifting. If it is helpful, draw a vertical line on your paper to make sure the center front edge is straight.

STEP 2

I chose to spread each section 2″ (5 cm) for fullness, but you can choose to add only 1″ (2.5 cm) if you don't want as much flare. Place the center front edge on the vertical line, spread each slash 2″ (5 cm) at the hem, and tape down the next section. Do this until all sections are spread evenly and are taped down. Trim the excess paper from underneath.

STEP 3

Follow steps 1 and 2 to create the back dress pattern.

* Label your new front and back pattern pieces the following: Front/Dropped Waist Dress/Size/Cut 1 on Fold; Back/Dropped Waist Dress/Size/Cut 1 on Fold

B (STEPS 1 AND 2)

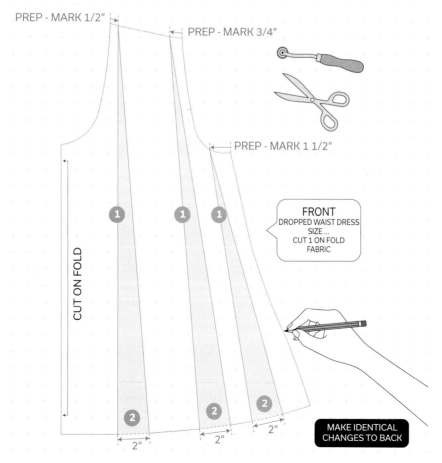

PREP - MARK 1/2"

PREP - MARK 3/4"

PREP - MARK 1 1/2"

CUT ON FOLD

FRONT
DROPPED WAIST DRESS
SIZE ...
CUT 1 ON FOLD
FABRIC

2" 2" 2"

MAKE IDENTICAL CHANGES TO BACK

SLEEVE AND CUFF MODIFICATION

To make the cuff, measure around your wrist and add 3" (7.6 cm) (1/2" will be the seam allowance). Cut 2 rectangles to this width by 6" (15.2 cm) long (deep) from the ribbing fabric, either the dress knit or specialty ribbed knit designed for this purpose. Fold each cuff RS together so the 6" (15.2 cm) ends meet and stitch to form a loop. Turn to the RS and fold in half, WS facing. Instead of hemming the sleeve, slip the cuff over the end of the sleeve, aligning raw edges. Stitch the cuff to the sleeve, stretching the cuff if needed as you sew. Press to the RS.

Other options: You can play around with the length of the sleeve before adding the cuff; you can change the depth of the cuff; you can slash-and-spread the sleeve for more drama; or you can slash-and-spread the sleeve and finish the hem with elastic instead of a cuff.

RUFFLED BOTTOM

STEP 1

Measure the hem width of the dress front. You will use this measurement to draft your ruffle. Multiply the width of the front hem by 1.5. Use that number on the next step.

STEP 2

Create a rectangle that measures the number you calculated above for the length by however deep you want the ruffle to be. Remember that the length of the dress includes the ruffle; check where you want this to fall on your body. I used 10" (25.4 cm) for the depth of my ruffle. Add a ¾" (1.9 cm) hem allowance to the bottom and a ⅜" (1 cm) allowance to the top edge. Cut your ruffle pattern piece. Draw the foldline at one short end (C).

- Label your new piece with the following: Ruffle/ Dropped Waist Dress/Size/Cut 2 on Fold

C

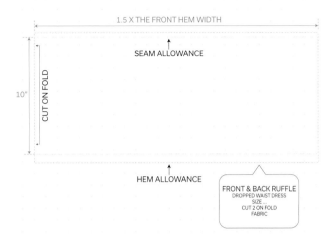

SEWING INSTRUCTIONS

You will attach the front to the back at the shoulders, apply the NECKBAND, and sew the side seams and sleeve just as in the Fitted Tee instructions, but finish the sleeve with the Cuff instead of a hem. Sew the side seams of the ruffle, gather the top edge, and attach the ruffle to the hem of the dress. Finish the hem of the ruffle by turning it under ¾" (1.9 cm) and stitching.

gathered waist t-shirt dress

A t-shirt dress is a great addition to your wardrobe. This t-shirt dress has waist gathers that make it cute and comfy to wear. Decide how long you want your t-shirt dress to be: mini, knee-length, or longer.

Pieces being modified: Fitted Tee *Front, Back,* and *Sleeve*

Additional pattern pieces needed: Fitted Tee *Neckband,* Pencil Skirt *Front* and *Back*

Fabric recommendations: spandex jersey / linen knit blends / ribbed knits / bamboo knits / modal knits

PREP

Place the Fitted Tee FRONT and BACK on new paper and draw a vertical line that is the length you want for the dress. Trace the front and back patterns and transfer notches. Transfer the waistline marking using your tracing wheel and draw it in (A).

A

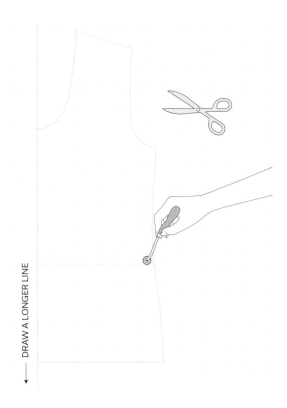

DRAW A LONGER LINE

FRONT AND BACK

STEP 1

Remove the Fitted Tee front base pattern once traced. Grab the Pencil Skirt FRONT pattern and align the skirt waistline on the waistline of the tee. The skirt waistline has a slight curve, so align it close to the center front, then align the skirt hip to the hemline of the tee at the side seam. Trace the skirt front onto the paper: center front, side seam, and hem. Mark a short notch and write "hip" on the dress pattern where the hipline of the skirt hits the dress pattern at the side seam (B)

- Note: Your skirt may extend further than the vertical line at the center front—that is OK. Just make sure that it extends the same distance all along the length, measuring to the vertical line marked on the paper.

STEP 2

Repeat step 1 for the back (you won't be using the vent). Make sure to also transfer the skirt hip notch onto the back. Double-check that it matches the front by measuring from the waist to the skirt hip notch you made on the front dress. The distance needs to be the same on your back pattern.

CREATING THE GATHERS

STEP 1

On the new front pattern piece, measure down 3" (7.6 cm) from the underarm and make a mark. We will be gathering between this mark and the hip notch. Now measure the distance between those notches and round up to the nearest whole number. Divide this number by 3. Use that figure and measure from the underarm, make a hashmark, then move the same amount toward the hip and make another hashmark.

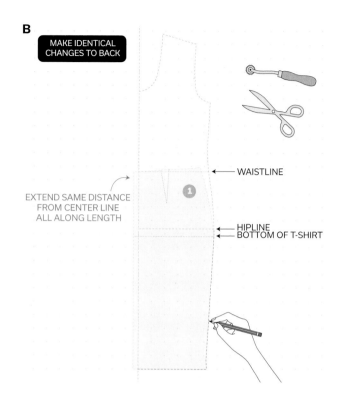

B

MAKE IDENTICAL CHANGES TO BACK

WAISTLINE

EXTEND SAME DISTANCE FROM CENTER LINE ALL ALONG LENGTH

HIPLINE
BOTTOM OF T-SHIRT

Draw four slash lines from the center front to the side seam on the front of the dress; one at the hip, one at each hashmark, and one at the 3" (7.6 cm) mark. Note: Make sure that your waistline is clearly marked on your pattern. Mark the slash lines on the back as for the front.

STEP 2

You will add a total of 8" (20.3 cm) to the waist for the ruched waistline.

- Note: Make sure to mark each section with a number so you don't lose track, and it may be helpful to mark the edge that is at the center front.
- Cut out the front and back dress patterns.

STEP 3

Cut the slash lines across the patterns from edge to edge. Place the patterns onto large pieces of new paper. Tape down the top of the pattern. Spread each slashed section apart, in the correct order, by 2" (5 cm), being sure you have the center front of each piece in the correct orientation. Tape the edges down. Connect the spaces at the center front and side seam. Do the same slash and spread for the back. Trace off the finished dress pattern front and back and cut out.

SEWING INSTRUCTIONS

Start by gathering the side seams on the front and back by making two rows of gathering stitches in the seam allowance. Pull the bobbin threads until the front and back both match lengthwise. Continue sewing the shoulders, sleeve, side seams, neckband, and hem following the instructions for your Fitted Tee base pattern. Make sure to use a narrow zigzag stitch or your serger for this garment so you don't pop stitches when pulling it on.

C (STEPS 1 - 3)

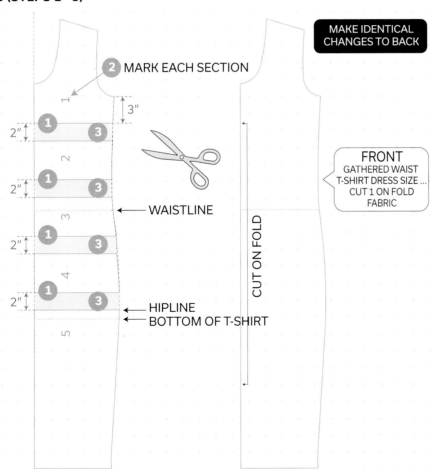

MAKE IDENTICAL CHANGES TO BACK

2 MARK EACH SECTION

3"

2"

2"

WAISTLINE

2"

2"

HIPLINE
BOTTOM OF T-SHIRT

CUT ON FOLD

FRONT
GATHERED WAIST
T-SHIRT DRESS SIZE ...
CUT 1 ON FOLD
FABRIC

turtleneck

I love a great fitted turtleneck; it can be so chic with trousers and skirts. For this top, you'll do a simple modification to the Fitted Tee.

Pieces being modified: Fitted Tee *Front*

Additional pattern pieces needed: Fitted Tee *Back, Sleeve*

Fabric recommendations: jersey knits / cotton knits / ribbed knits

STEP 1

Trace the FRONT pattern, except the neckline. Trace the neckline of the BACK onto the front. Mark down from the front neckline at the center front by ⅝" (1.5 cm) and blend the neckline to this lower depth, using a curved ruler (A).

STEP 2

Measure the front and back necklines on the pattern pieces, minus the seam allowances. (This will be half of the total measurement of the neckline.) Draw a rectangle the width measured plus a ⅜" (1 cm) seam allowance and decide on the height of your turtleneck. Make the rectangle's width double the height you want. Mark a foldline at one short end (B).

- Label this piece Collar/Turtleneck/size/Cut 1 on Fold

SEWING INSTRUCTIONS

Sew the shoulder seams, sleeves, and side seams just as for the Fitted Tee base pattern. For the turtleneck piece, fold in half WS together and stitch onto the neckline. Place the seam at the top's center back. I strongly suggest using a narrow zigzag stitch or your serger so you can get the greatest stretch at the neck.

A

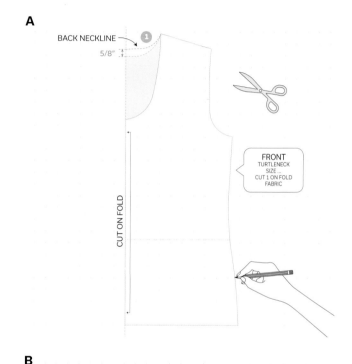

B

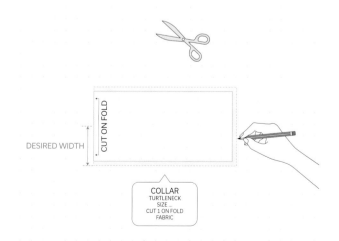

THE WRAP DRESS
wrap top with peplum

Flattering, so wearable, and sexy—that is what comes to mind when I look at this top. Make your peplum as short or long as you want. You can also choose to add length to the front and back bodice and omit the peplum for a clean look.

Pieces being modified: Wrap Dress *Skirt Front* and *Skirt Back*

Additional pattern pieces needed: Wrap Dress *Front Bodice* and *Back Bodice, Sleeve, Neck Binding, Left Side Tie* and *Right Side Tie*

Fabric recommendations: Spandex jersey / linen knit blends / ribbed knits / bamboo knits / modal knits

A

STEP 1

Starting at one side seam, measure down from the waistline on the SKIRT 8" (20.3 cm), move over a few inches and measure 8" (20.3 cm) down again, and continue, making hashmarks at each spot, until you reach the other side seam. Connect the dashes. Now trace the top part of the skirt, side seams, and peplum hem you just marked, being sure to add ⅜" (1 cm) for a hem allowance. Cut out your new peplum piece and transfer the center front/center back line; add a new side seam notch in the peplum (A).

- Note: When you fold your skirt along the foldline to cut the back on the fold, one edge will be shorter; this is to accommodate for the wrap. This is also true for the peplum. Refer to the Cutting Layout for the Wrap Dress (page 174) to see how to cut this piece.

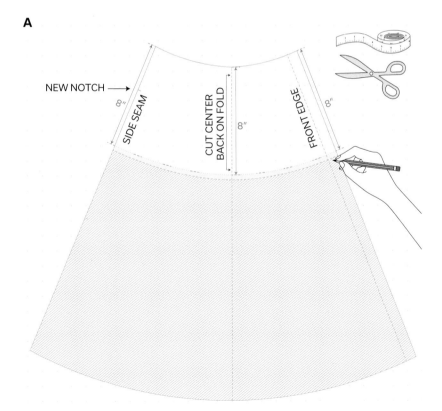

NEW NOTCH → 8" SIDE SEAM CUT CENTER BACK ON FOLD 8" FRONT EDGE 8"

STEP 2

Fold along the center front/center back line and draw a line where the shorter edge falls. Now fold the pattern in half, meeting the line you just drew; fold once more to the edge line, then fold one more time. The crease lines you folded are the slash lines; draw them in. From the hem of the peplum cut up to but not through the waistline, creating a hinge. Be sure you do not slash along the center foldline or the edge line.

STEP 3

On new paper, draw a vertical line at least 12" (30.5 cm) long. Now draw a horizontal line the same length at the end of the vertical line, creating an "L". From the corner, draw a 45-degree angle line and make sure it is accurate.

STEP 4

Place the peplum's center front/center back on the 45-degree line and tape it in place. Place the side seam that has the notch on the horizontal line; make sure you align the edge line you drew on the peplum to the horizontal guideline. Tape in place. Now place the front edge of the peplum on the vertical line. Spread and tape down the other slashed lines as evenly as possible.

STEP 5

Connect the spaces at the waistline and hem between the slashes and cut out the new pattern.
Label the pattern with the following: Peplum Wrap Top/Size/Cut 2 for Front, Cut 1 on Fold for Back

SEWING INSTRUCTIONS

Follow the Wrap Dress base pattern instructions.
The only difference here is the peplum versus skirt.

B (STEPS 2 - 5)

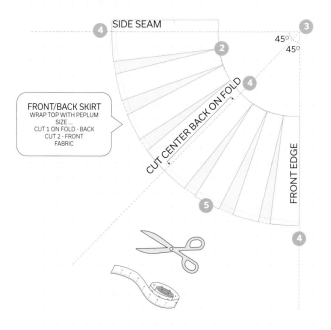

FRONT/BACK SKIRT
WRAP TOP WITH PEPLUM
SIZE ...
CUT 1 ON FOLD - BACK
CUT 2 - FRONT
FABRIC

SIDE SEAM

45°
45°

CUT CENTER BACK ON FOLD

FRONT EDGE

wrap dress with ruffle

Let's add some flare with a ruffled bottom on your Wrap Dress skirt! This can be extended to a maxi-length or shortened to mini-length.

Pieces being modified: Wrap Dress *Skirt Front* and *Skirt Back*

Additional pattern pieces needed: Wrap Dress *Bodice Front* and *Bodice Back, Sleeve, Left Tie* and *Right Tie, Neck Binding*

Fabric recommendations: spandex jersey / linen knit blends / ribbed knits / bamboo knits / modal knits

PREP

Decide how long you want the dress's main skirt to fall. Like the Dropped Waist T-Shirt Dress (page 116), keep in mind that the entire length will include the 6″ (15.2 cm) ruffle you're going to add; measure down from the waist to however long you want the dress to hit on your body before the ruffle. Add a ½″ (1.2 cm) seam allowance. Mark the length on your skirt pattern the same way as in step 1 for the Wrap Top with Peplum (page 127) and draw the new hemline (A).

Trace off the top part of the skirt front and back onto new paper. If you've trimmed away the existing side seam notch from the base pattern because you've shortened the shirt, add a new notch at the side seam and transfer the center front/center back line. Cut out the pattern (B).

- Label the new pattern piece with the following: Skirt/Wrap Dress with Ruffle/Size/Cut 2 for Front, Cut 1 on Fold for Back

A

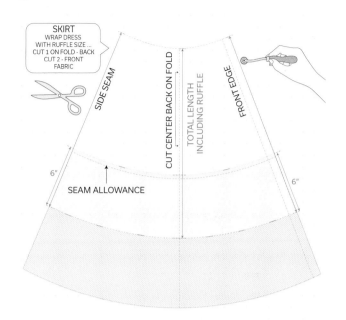

B

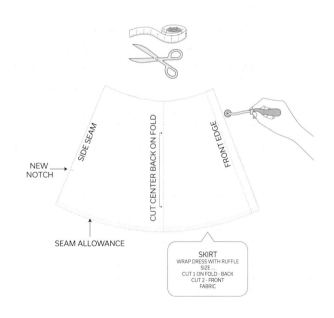

SKIRT RUFFLE

STEP 1

For the front ruffle, measure the entire width of the bottom edge of the skirt and multiply it by 1.5. Note the number. Now draw a rectangle that measures 6″ (15.2 cm) wide and make the length the number you calculated. Add ½″ (1.2 cm) seam allowance to the top and a 1″ (2.5 cm) hem allowance to the bottom.

- Label the new pattern piece with the following: Front Ruffle/Wrap Dress with Ruffle/Size/Cut 2

STEP 2

For the back ruffle, measure the width of the bottom edge of the skirt from the center back line to the side seam and multiply it by 1.5. Note the number. Now draw a rectangle that measures 6″ (15.2 cm) wide and make the length the number you calculated. Mark the foldline at one short end. Add ½″ (1.2 cm) seam allowance to the top and a 1″ (2.5 cm) hem allowance to the bottom.

- Label the new pattern piece with the following: Back Ruffle/Wrap Dress with Ruffle/Size/Cut 1 on Fold

SEWING INSTRUCTIONS

Use the Wrap Dress base pattern instructions. The only differences are the the shortened sleeve and the ruffle at the bottom of the skirt. If you want the short sleeve, see the Empire Button-Up with Ruffle (page 76) for instructions on how to alter the pattern. To add the ruffle, gather the top edge of the ruffle and attach it to the skirt's bottom edge, then finish the hem of the ruffle.

C (STEPS 1 AND 2)

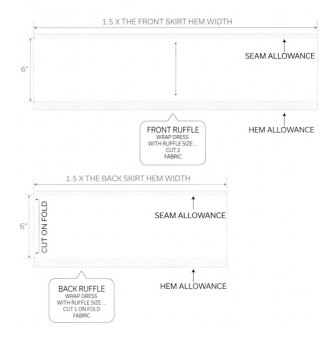

THE CAMISOLE
slip dress

The slip dress is a must-have. It is sexy and can be worn so many ways all year round, depending on how you style it. This is a great way of learning how to combine two patterns to create a new look. In this case, we take the Camisole and Pencil Skirt to create a slip dress.

Pieces being modified: Camisole *Front* and *Back*

Additional pattern pieces needed: Camisole *Front* and *Back*, *Straps*, *Front Facing*, *Back Facing*, Pencil Skirt *Front* and *Back*

Fabric recommendations: silks or silky types / chambray / rayon prints or solids / linen and linen blends / crepe

PREP

Start by extending the camisole's waistline marking to the side seams to both ends on the front and back patterns. Fold the Camisole FRONT and BACK in half, so the side seams meet. Fold a large piece of paper in half.

FRONT MODIFICATIONS
STEP 1

Place the folded front cami pattern onto the folded edge of your new paper. Trace the cami front to the waistline marking only. Transfer the dart, notches, and grainlines (A).

A

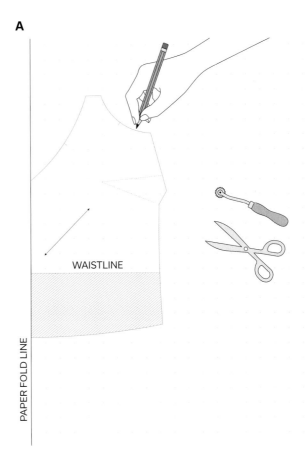

WAISTLINE

PAPER FOLD LINE

STEP 2

Place the Pencil Skirt FRONT pattern on the folded edge of the paper while placing the skirt's waistline edge to the cami waistline. The skirt waistline will not sit perfectly on the cami waistline, so align it such that the skirt's waistline/side seam is on the waistline of the camisole front. Trace the skirt side seam and hemline. Transfer the hip notch.

Measure from the waistline of the skirt front straight down to the hipline while the pattern is still in place; note this for later.

STEP 3

From the bottom dart leg on the side seam of the cami front, draw a straight line to where the skirt waistline hits the cami waistline; blend the line with a curved ruler. Make a notch at the waistline. Measure from the underarm to the top dart leg; note this for later. Using your tracing wheel, with the paper still folded in half, trace over the front dart and all notches. Unfold the paper and draw in the dart on the other side and the notches. Cut out the pattern.

- Label the new pattern with the following: Slip Dress/Front/Size/Cut 1 Fabric

B (STEPS 2 & 3)

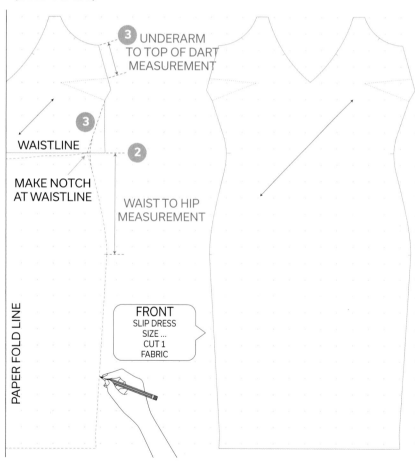

BACK MODIFICATIONS

STEP 1

Place the folded back cami pattern onto the folded edge of your new paper. Trace the cami back to the waistline marking. Transfer the notches and grainlines. Remove the pattern piece.

Measure down from the cami back's waistline the amount measured in step 2 above and make a mark, then draw a guideline across to mark the hipline level (C).

STEP 2

The back skirt pattern has a seam allowance on the center back, and you need to remove it. Draw a new line along the ⅜" (1 cm) seam allowance on the skirt BACK pattern (D).

C

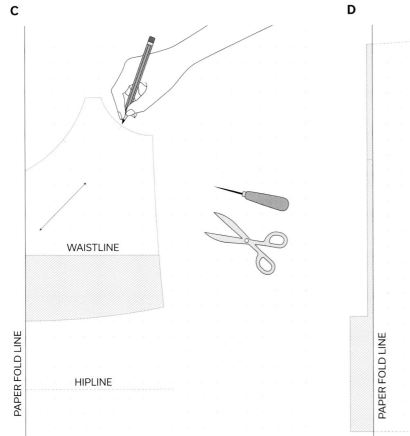

PAPER FOLD LINE

WAISTLINE

HIPLINE

D

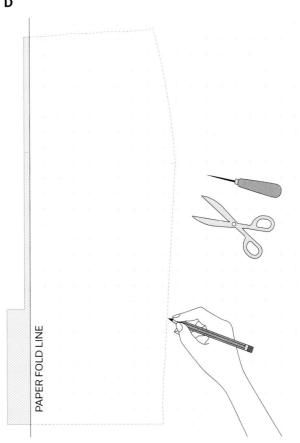

PAPER FOLD LINE

STEP 3

Align the marked seamline on the folded edge of the paper. The skirt back waistline will not sit perfectly on the cami waistline, so you need to align it so that the skirt's hipline is aligned with the hip marking you drew in step 1 above. Trace the skirt side seam and hemline. Transfer the hip notch. Remove the pattern piece.

STEP 4

Where the skirt hits the waistline of the cami at the side seam, measure in ½" (1.3 cm) and make a mark. Measure down from the cami back underarm the amount you measured in step 3 (Front Modifications), make another mark. Draw a line from this mark to the ½" (1.3 cm) mark you made at the waist. Using your French curve or hip curve ruler, blend from the ½" (1.3 cm) mark into the hip. Make a notch marking at the waistline.

You don't want any sharp points on the side seam at the waist, so use your French curve again to gently round off the waistline. Also blend in at the mark below the underarm.

Using your tracing wheel, with the paper still folded in half, trace over all back notches. Unfold the paper and draw in the markings.

- Label the new pattern with the following: Slip Dress/Back/Size/Cut 1 Fabric

E (STEPS 3 & 4)

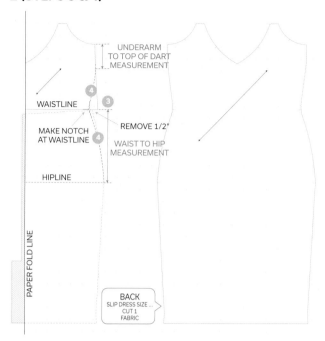

SEWING INSTRUCTIONS

Use the instructions for the base pattern Camisole to sew your slip dress. Make sure not to pull or let the dress hang off your sewing table, because bias cut garments tend to stretch. Take care when sewing and use a lot of pins. After sewing the slip dress but before finishing the hem, let the dress hang on a dress form or hanger for twenty-four hours before hemming to let the fabric relax on the bias.

jumpsuit

The jumpsuit is great for day and night, depending on your fabric choice. This is another way of learning how to combine two patterns for a new look. In this case, you combine the Camisole and Trouser patterns to create the jumpsuit. You have some cool design options like adding elastic to the Trouser hem or making the straps ties instead.

Pieces modified: Camisole *Front* and *Back*

Additional pieces needed: Camisole *Straps*, *Front* and *Back Facings*; Trouser *Front* and *Back*, *Pocket Bag*, *Pocket Facing*

Fabric recommendations: silks or silky types / chambray / rayon prints or solids / linen and linen blends / crepe

TROUSER FRONT MODIFICATIONS

On the Trouser FRONT, measure and mark a 1" (2.5 cm) line from the fly front extension's edge and fold it under to keep it out of the way. Pin the POCKET BAG in place along the trouser front and side. You need a reference point for where to add width. Fold the pant leg along the straight edge of the pocket bag, making sure the knee line and hipline match, and crease this fold. Draw a line to mark the crease (A).

A

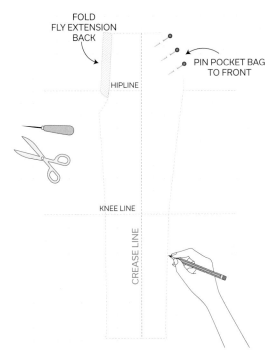

TROUSER BACK MODIFICATIONS

You will not sew the back darts on the trouser back; instead, you'll use the added fullness for the jumpsuit. Fold the trouser BACK pattern along the middle of the dart closest to the side seam, making sure that the knee line and hipline match. Crease this fold. Draw a line to mark the crease. This will ensure the grainlines stay intact on both the front and back trouser (B).

B

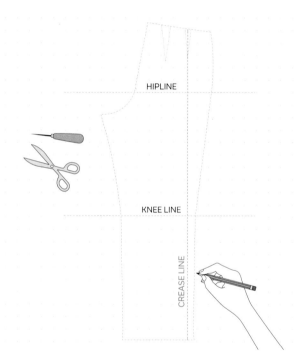

CAMI FRONT AND BACK MODIFICATIONS

STEP 1

On a new piece of paper, draw a vertical line to indicate the center back foldline. Fold the pattern piece in half and trace the cami BACK, stopping at the waistline marking, the same as for the slip dress. Transfer the notches, and square off the waistline from center back (C). Because this is a jumpsuit, we need to add length to accommodate movement and comfort. Measure down 1" (2.5 cm) below the waistline, and below that add ½" (1.3 cm) for a seam allowance. Draw in the center back foldline and cut out the pattern (D).

- Label your new pattern piece the following: Bodice Back/Jumpsuit/Size/Cut 1 on Fold

STEP 2

On a new piece of paper, draw a vertical line to indicate the center front foldline. Fold the pattern piece in half and trace the cami FRONT, stopping at the waistline marking, the same as for the back. Transfer the dart and notches and square off the waistline from the center front (E). Measure down 1" (2.5 cm) from the waistline, and below that add ½" (1.3 cm) for a seam allowance. Draw in the center front foldline and cut out the pattern (F).

- Label your new pattern piece the following: Bodice Front/Jumpsuit/Size/Cut 1 on Fold

STEP 3

Measure along the waistline of the front and back, including side seam allowances, and note each measurement.

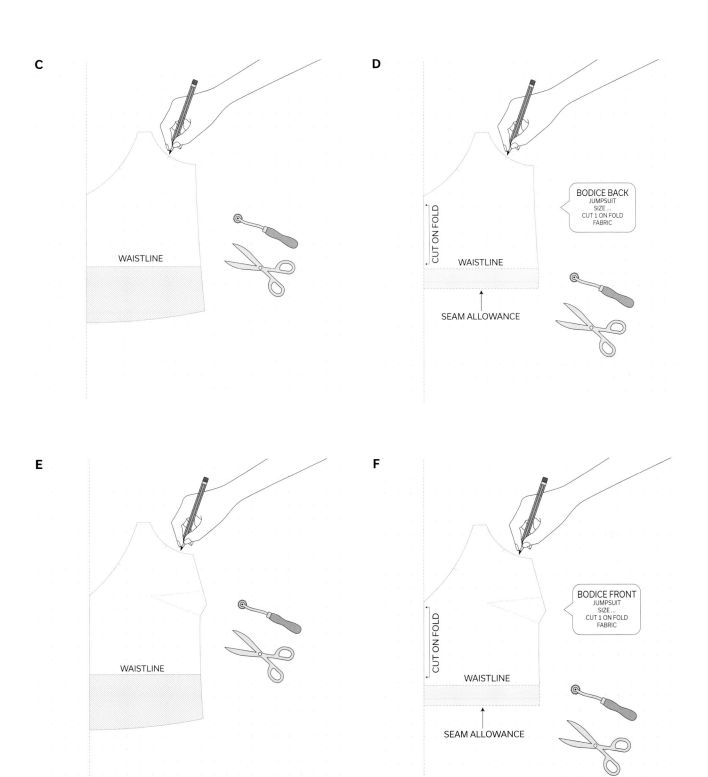

ADJUSTING BACK PANT WIDTH

STEP 1

Place the BACK trouser pattern on new paper. Extend the hipline and knee line markings to each edge and then onto the paper. Remove the back pattern and draw in the full lines as guides. Extend the lines well past the outseam so there is room to expand the pattern. Place the back pattern onto the paper again and makes sure the lines align. Weigh the pattern down to prevent movement.

Trace the inseam, the crotch, the waistline to the marked crease line, and the hem to the marked crease line. Make sure to transfer notches and the crease line. You can use your tracing wheel to mark it and then draw it in. Measure in and mark the ⅜" (1 cm) seam allowance along the center back of the pant.

STEP 2

Measure the entire back waistline beginning from the center back seamline. Note the measurement. The trouser back waistline needs to match the modified cami back waistline. Subtract the trouser back waistline measurement from the cami back waistline measurement from step 3, Cami Front and Back Modifications, and note the difference.

STEP 3

Measure from the crease line toward the side seam at the trouser waistline the amount you need to add and make a mark on the paper. Do the same at the hem. Move the trouser pattern so that the crease line aligns with the marks you just made at the waistline and hem.

- Note: Make sure that after moving the trouser pattern the hipline and knee line are still aligned.

G (STEPS 1 - 4)

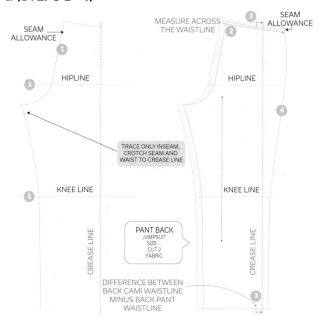

STEP 4

Continue tracing the new waistline, outseam, and hem. Transfer notches. Add a ½" (1.3 cm) seam allowance to the waistline. Cut out the new pattern.

- Label the new pattern piece the following: Pant Back/Jumpsuit/Size/Cut 2

ADJUSTING FRONT PANT WIDTH

Adjust the front trouser pattern by following steps 1 through 4 of Adjusting Back Pant Width, above, making the same adjustments you made to the back—with one difference. You will be keeping the front pleat, so mark those lines on the paper. In step 2, first close the trouser front's pleat by folding one line to meet the other, then measure the entire front waistline beginning at the center front seamline. Unfold the pleat after measuring. Subtract this measurement from the cami front waistline measurement and add the difference to the front pant as for the back.

Unpin the pocket bag from the trouser front. Finish tracing the waistline, outseam, and hem. You will use the pockets for the jumpsuit (H).

- Label your new piece the following: Pant Front/ Jumpsuit/Size/Cut 2

H (AS FRONT, STEPS 1 - 4)

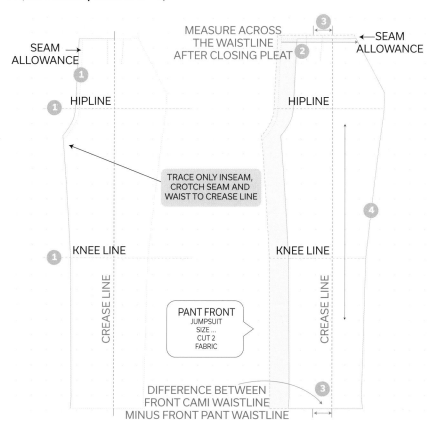

SEAM ALLOWANCE

MEASURE ACROSS THE WAISTLINE AFTER CLOSING PLEAT

← SEAM ALLOWANCE

HIPLINE

HIPLINE

TRACE ONLY INSEAM, CROTCH SEAM AND WAIST TO CREASE LINE

KNEE LINE

KNEE LINE

CREASE LINE

CREASE LINE

PANT FRONT
JUMPSUIT
SIZE ...
CUT 2
FABRIC

DIFFERENCE BETWEEN FRONT CAMI WAISTLINE MINUS FRONT PANT WAISTLINE

POCKET AND POCKET FACING ADJUSTMENTS

Because you have added a ½" (1.3 cm) seam allowance to the top of the trouser front waistline, you need to trace the pocket bag and the pocket facing onto new paper and add a ½" (1.3 cm) seam allowance to each waistline (I).

- Label your new pattern pieces the following: Pocket Bag/Jumpsuit/Cut 2; Pocket Facing/Jumpsuit/Cut 2

I

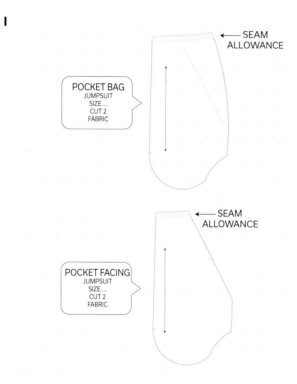

SEAM ALLOWANCE

POCKET BAG
JUMPSUIT
SIZE ...
CUT 2
FABRIC

SEAM ALLOWANCE

POCKET FACING
JUMPSUIT
SIZE ...
CUT 2
FABRIC

TIE (OPTIONAL)

If you would like to create a fabric belt for your jumpsuit, measure your waist and multiply it by 1.5 or 2, if you want a longer belt. Now draw a rectangle that measures the total length by 4" (10.2 cm) wide. Mark the foldline at one short end; you can angle the other end if you prefer. To sew, fold lengthwise with RS together and stitch, leaving an opening for turning. Turn, press, and stitch the opening closed.

- Label your pattern the following: Tie/Jumpsuit/Cut 1 on Fold

STRAPS (OPTIONAL)

Like the Cropped Cami with Ruffle hack (page 145), it's easy to add tie straps to your jumpsuit. Simply cut four straps instead of two—as long as you'd like—sew them on to front and back and tie at the shoulders when you wear the garment.

SEWING INSTRUCTIONS

Follow the Camisole instructions (page 133) to sew the jumpsuit top, omitting the hem. Sew the jumpsuit bottoms following trouser instructions for side seam, inseam and crotch, and then attach to the top at the waist, RS together. Press the waistline seam allowances up toward the top and stitch through them all around the waist to create a casing for elastic, leaving a 1" (2.5 cm) opening to insert the elastic. Insert the elastic, overlap and stitch the ends, stitch closed the opening, and finish the hem of the pants. If you want to make your hems gathered with elastic, make a casing at the bottom in the same manner as you would for the waist, insert elastic, and stitch the opening closed.

cropped cami with ruffle

This is a quick and easy hack to add a ruffle to the bottom of the camisole with no changes made to the base camisole pattern.

Pieces needed: Camisole *Front, Back, Straps, Front Facing,* and *Back Facing*

Fabric recommendations: silks or silky types / chambray / rayon prints or solids / linen and linen blends / crepe

DRAFT THE RUFFLE

Draft a rectangle for the ruffle by measuring the FRONT and BACK hemline of the cami. Add both measurements together and multiply the total by 1.5. Draw a rectangle that measures that total length by however wide you want the ruffle. Add a ½″ (1.3 cm) seam allowance to the cami hem and ½″ (1.3 cm) to the top of the ruffle.

To add further flair, cut four of the cami's STRAPS extra-long, sew them to the cami front and back, and tie them at the shoulder (A)!

SEWING INSTRUCTIONS

Sew this up using your Camisole base instructions. Sew your ruffle side seams together, gather, and attach to the cami hem, then finish the hem of the ruffle.

A

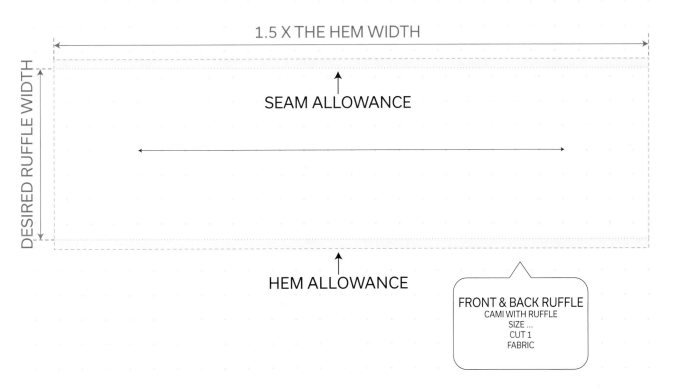

1.5 X THE HEM WIDTH

DESIRED RUFFLE WIDTH

SEAM ALLOWANCE

HEM ALLOWANCE

FRONT & BACK RUFFLE
CAMI WITH RUFFLE
SIZE ...
CUT 1
FABRIC

THE DUSTER
kimono-inspired jacket

The Duster jacket base pattern changes drastically according to the fabric you choose. If you use a stiffer fabric like a lightweight wool, quilted fabric, denim, or brocade, you will have a beautiful, structured jacket. Using a flowing fabric like a silky type, lightweight cotton, chiffon, or even a knit will give a more traditional kimono-inspired drape and look. It's very easy to change the hemline and vary the length of the sleeves to change up the look too. Here are two quick and easy hacks!

- **OPTION 1:** Using the Duster length as-is, shorten the NECKBAND by 10" (25.4 cm), finish the ends, and attach the new neckband following the base pattern sewing instructions.

- **OPTION 2:** Measure from your shoulder to your waist and shorten the Duster front and back pattern by transferring that length to the base pattern. Trace the new FRONT and BACK onto new paper. Now let's add patch pockets to the front:

Notions: lightweight interfacing

STEP 1

Draw a box for the pocket that measures 6" × 7" (15.2 cm × 17.8 cm). You can play with the size to suit your style. Add seam allowance of ½" (1.3 cm) to the sides and bottom and 1" (2.5 cm) to the top.

STEP 2

For the flaps, draw a box that measures 6" × 4" (15.2 cm x 10.2 cm) and add a ½" (1.3 cm) seam allowance all the way around.

- Label your pocket pattern pieces the following: Patch Pocket/Cut 2; Patch Pocket Flaps/Cut 4 Fabric, Cut 2 Interfacing

SEWING INSTRUCTIONS

Follow the instructions given for the Duster base pattern (see page 61).

style guide

RULE'S DON'T MATTER

Yep, you read that right. I have never been one to follow "fashion rules." I wear white after Labor Day, I wear maxi-length skirts and dresses even though I am only five feet, four inches tall. And I don't care whatsoever about mixing prints, wearing loud bold colors, crazy prints, or what others may or may not think is appropriate. I guess I have always been a rebel, but the fact is that you should wear what makes *you* feel good—and if, in wearing that, you feel confident, then others will see that confidence too. Now, obviously there are a few things to consider that are not rules, like proportion and fit, but fashion sewing is truly about making what *you* like and want to wear.

MIXING PRINTS

Fun, fun, fun! This isn't something everyone is comfortable with, so I challenge you to look beyond the traditional standards of mixing prints and venture out. There are the classic prints, of course, like polka dots, plaids, stripes, florals, and animal prints that go together very well and can be worn all year round. Then there is nontraditional print mixing like florals and checks or two different types of plaids in colors that are not at all coordinating.

If you are new to print mixing, start with two prints. Adding a third print can be tricky if you follow those "rules" I mentioned before—but if you don't, mix away! Try to keep your prints to varying scales for interest. For example, you could do a small print for your top, a medium print for your bottom, and a large-scale print for your jacket.

Another thing to consider if you are new to print mixing is to keep your prints in the same tonal range, or use two different prints in the same colorway.

FABRIC DOES MATTER!

If you don't choose the right fabric, your garment can quickly go from fab to drab. Learning about fabric and how to match it to your me-makes is something that takes many people a long time to learn. Using a swatch book to help you learn fabric content and characteristics is a great way to start making the right choices. Looking at content labels of your ready-to-wear garments is also a way to learn what certain content combinations feel like so that when you are shopping for fabric and see similar fabric contents, you can get an idea of how it will look and drape.

Here is the thing: you can change the shape of a pattern by simply using a fabric that holds shape and has structure versus a flowing, soft, drapey fabric. The garment is the same, but it will look very different once sewn and worn. That makes sewing exciting and creative. Just remember that if a pattern calls for a woven, use a woven—and the same goes for knits. When a pattern is designed for a knit fabric, it is often designed with negative ease because the fabric stretches. If you were to cut a pattern that was designed for a knit out of a woven fabric, you would not be able to get into it. That doesn't mean you can't ever do it, it just means you need to know what modifications you need to make for it to work, like adding a zipper and wearing ease.

You will see much of what I have written about in the inspiration looks, and I hope that seeing how just seven patterns can be transformed into eighteen modifications and then turned into a total of more than one hundred looks inspires you to think beyond the pattern and gives you the confidence to expand your mind and your wardrobe.

100+
INSPI-
RATION
LOOKS

MAKE IT YOURS WITH MIMI G

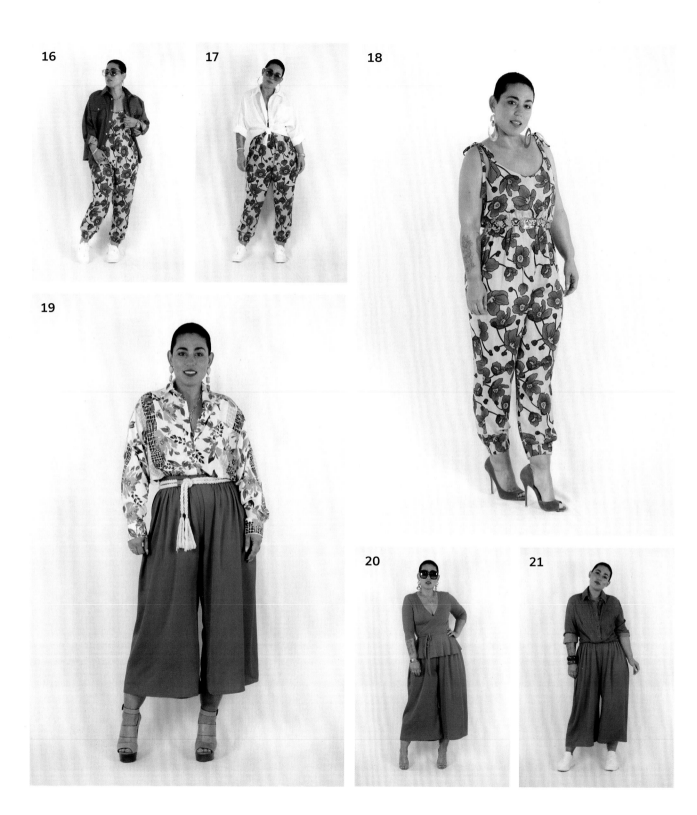

22

23

24

25

26

27

MAKE IT YOURS WITH MIMI G

37

38

39

40

41

42

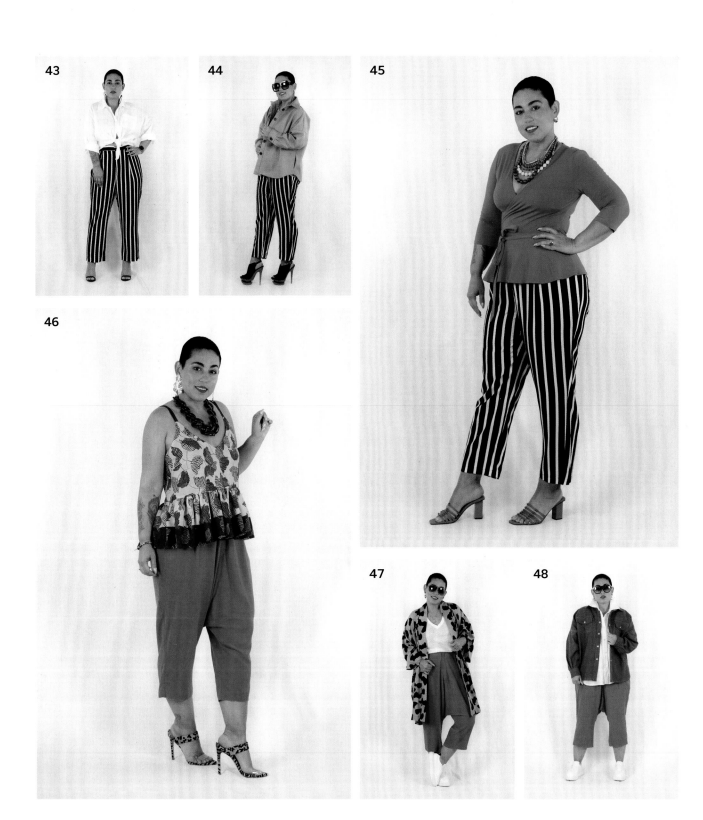

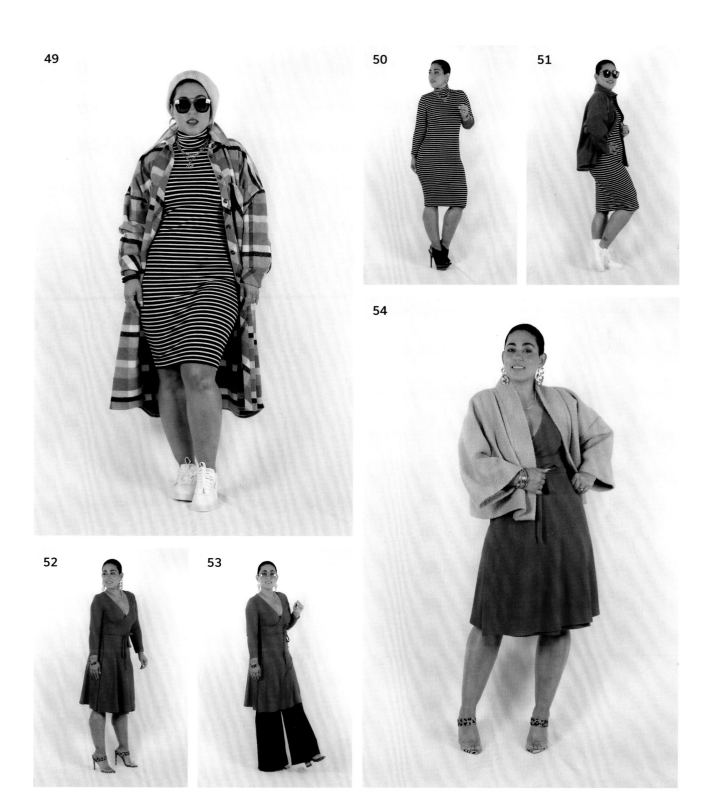

49

50

51

54

52

53

MAKE IT YOURS WITH MIMI G

61

62

63

64

65

66

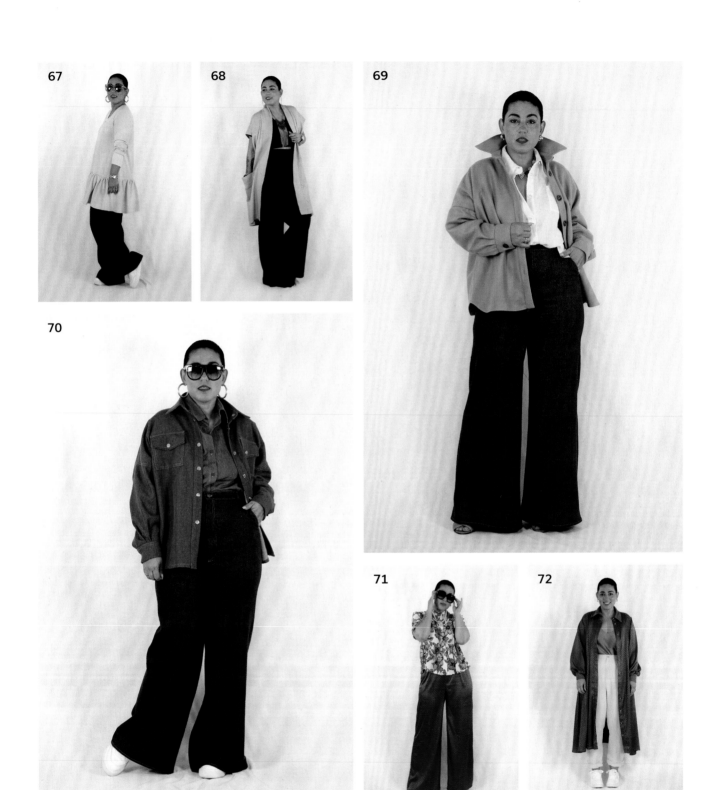

MAKE IT YOURS WITH MIMI G

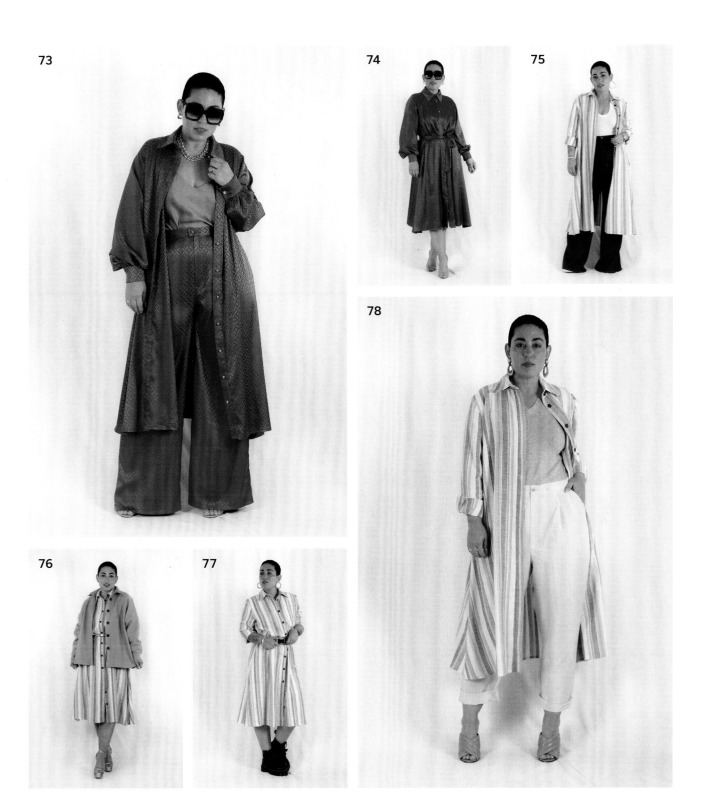

73

74

75

78

76

77

79

80

81

83

82

84

85

86

87

88

89

90

91

92

93

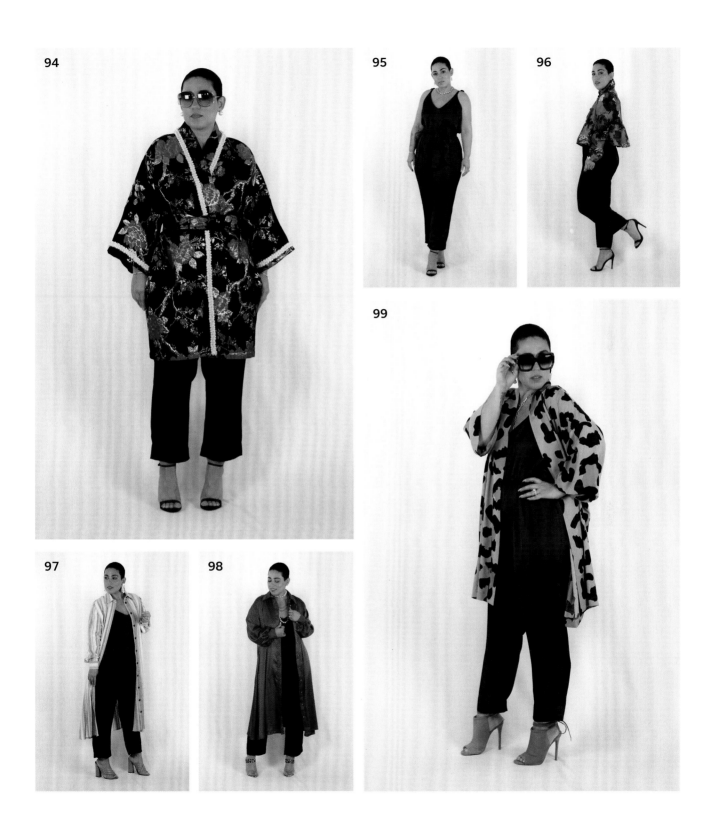

94

95

96

99

97

98

106

107

108

109

100+ inspiration looks: guide

1. Duster, Camisole, and denim Pencil Skirt in corduroy
2. Short Shacket hack in white cotton and denim Pencil Skirt in corduroy
3. Button up shirt and denim Pencil Skirt
4. Cropped Cami with ruffle hack and denim Pencil Skirt
5. Shacket hack in rayon print, Full Gathered Skirt short
6. Camisole, Full Gathered Skirt short
7. Empire Button-up Shirt with ruffle, Full Gathered Skirt short
8. Short Duster hack, Empire Button-up with ruffle hack, and Pencil Skirt
9. Short Shacket hack, Camisole, and Pencil Skirt
10. U-neck T-shirt, A-line Skirt
11. Short Shacket hack in cotton, u-neck t-shirt, A-line Skirt
12. Cropped Cami with ruffle hack and ties hack, A-line Skirt
13. Empire Button-up Shirt hack made longer for a dropped waist, Trousers
14. Empire Button-up Shirt hack made longer for a dropped waist
15. Empire Button-up Shirt hack made longer for a dropped waist, Wide Leg Pants hack
16. Camisole and Trouser hack turned Jumpsuit, short Shacket in denim
17. Camisole and Trouser hack turned Jumpsuit, short Shacket hack in cotton
18. Camisole and Trouser hack turned Jumpsuit
19. Short Shacket hack in rayon print, Palazzo Pants
20. Wrap Top with Peplum hack, Palazzo Pants
21. Button-up shirt, Palazzo Pants
22. Wrap Top with Peplum hack, Full Gathered Skirt hack long
23. Turtleneck hack, Full Gathered Skirt hack long
24. Empire Button-up with ruffle and long sleeves, Full Gathered Skirt hack long
25. Wrap top with peplum hack, A-line skirt
26. V-neck tee, A-line Skirt
27. Short Shacket hack in cotton, A-line skirt
28. Cropped T-shirt hack, Palazzo Pants hack
29. Turtlneck hack, Palazzo Pants
30. Camisole, Palazzo Pants hack
31. Wrap Top hack without peplum, Full Gathered Skirt hack short
32. Camisole, Full Gathered Skirt hack short
33. Short Shacket hack in cotton, Full Gathered Skirt hack short
34. Wrap Dress with ruffle
35. Wrap Dress with ruffle, Duster hack short
36. Wrap Dress with ruffle
37. Wrap Top with Peplum hack, Palazzo Pants hack
38. Camisole, Palazzo Pants hack
39. Button-up Shirt, Palazzo Pants hack
40. Slip Dress hack
41. Duster long, Slip Dress hack
42. Slip Dress hack
43. Short Shacket hack in cotton, Trousers
44. Short Shacket hack, Trousers
45. Wrap Dress hack in knit fabric, basic Trousers
46. Camisole hack with ruffle, drop crotch pants
47. Drop crotch pants, T-shirt, Duster long
48. Short Shacket hack in denim, short Shacket hack in cotton, Drop Crotch Pants
49. Long Shacket hack, T-shirt Dress hack with Turtleneck
50. T-shirt Dress hack with Turtleneck
51. Short Shacket hack in denim, T-shirt Dress hack with Turtleneck
52. Basic Wrap Dress
53. Wrap Dress, Wide Leg Trouser hack
54. Wrap Dress, Duster hack short

55. Wrap Top hack without peplum, basic Pencil Skirt
56. Short Shacket hack, basic Pencil Skirt
57. Shacket hack long, T-shirt, basic Pencil Skirt
58. Short Shacket hack in cotton, T-shirt, basic Pencil Skirt
59. Short Shacket hack in cotton, basic Trousers
60. Empire Waist Button-up with ruffle hack, basic Trousers
61. Empire Waist Button-up with ruffle and long sleeves hack, basic Trousers
62. Dropped Waist T-shirt hack without ruffle, basic Trousers
63. Dropped waist T-shirt Dress hack, short Shacket hack in denim
64. Dropped waist T-shirt Dress hack
65. Dropped waist T-shirt Dress hack, long Shacket hack
66. Dropped waist T-shirt Dress hack
67. Dropped waist dress T-shirt hack, wide leg Trousers
68. Sleeveless Duster hack, T-shirt, Wide Leg Trouser hack
69. Short Shacket hack, Wide Leg Trouser hack, short Shacket hack in cotton
70. Short Shacket hack in denim, Wide Leg Trouser hack

71. Empire Waist Button-up with ruffle hack, Wide Leg Trouser hack
72. Button-up Shirtdress hack, Camisole, basic Trouser
73. Button-up Shirtdress hack, Camisole, Wide Leg Trouser hack
74. Button-up Shirtdress hack
75. Button-up Shirtdress hack, T-shirt, Wide Leg Trouser hack
76. Button-up Shirtdress hack, short Shacket hack
77. Button-up Shirtdress hack
78. Button-up Shirtdress hack, T-shirt, basic Trousers
79. Wrap Top hack without peplum, Drop Crotch Pants
80. Short Shacket hack in denim, T-shirt dropped waist without ruffle hack, Drop Crotch Pants
81. Duster long, T-shirt, Drop Crotch Pants
82. Empire Button-up hack with ruffle, Drop Crotch Pants
83. Long Shacket hack, T-shirt, Drop Crocth Pants
84. Slip Dress
85. Short Shacket hack in denim, Slip Dress hack
86. Short Shacket hack in cotton, Slip Dress
87. T-shirt, Slip Dress hack
88. Duster, Slip Dress hack

89. Duster, T-shirt, Gathered Waist Dress hack
90. T-shirt Gathered Dress hack, short Shacket hack in cotton
91. T-shirt Gathered Dress hack
92. T-shirt Gathered Dress hack, short Shacket hack in rayon
93. Shacket hack short with Gathered Waist T-shirt Dress
94. Jumpsuit hack, Duster
95. Jumpsuit hack
96. Jumpsuit hack, Empire Button-up shirt with ruffle hack
97. Button-up Shirtdress hack, Jumpsuit hack
98. Button-up Shirtdress hack, Jumpsuit hack
99. Duster, Jumpsuit hack
100. Short Shacket hack in denim, T-shirt, basic Trousers
101. Turtleneck hack, basic Trouser
102. Basic Button-up and Trousers
103. Camisole, basic Trouser
104. Duster, basic Trouser
105. Long Shacket hack, short Shacket hack in cotton, basic Trouser
106. Camisole with ruffle hack, basic Trouser
107. Shacket hack short in rayon print, basic Trousers
108. Wrap Dress long hack
109. Sleeveless Duster hack with tie belt

cutting layouts

THE BUTTON-UP

Fold fabric in half and cut all pattern pieces. Pattern pieces 1, 2, 5, and 6 are cut on the fold.

45" (115 cm) wide fabric

XXS to S

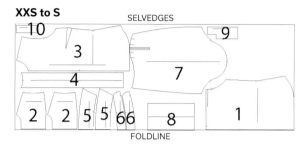

M to 2XL

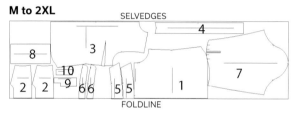

60" (115 cm) wide fabric

XXS to S

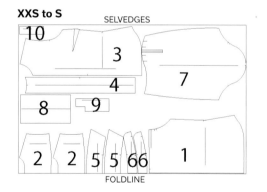

M to 2XL

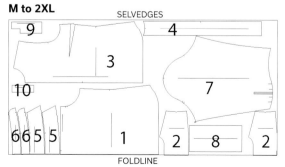

THE TROUSERS

Fold fabric in half and cut all pattern pieces.

45" (115 cm) wide fabric

XXS to S

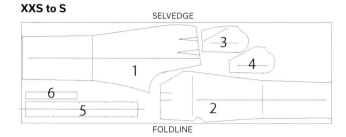

M to 2XL

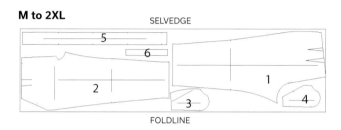

60" (150 cm) wide fabric

XXS to S

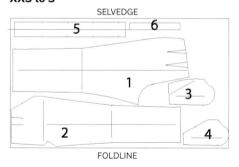

M to 2XL

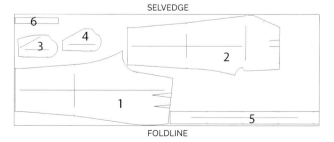

THE PENCIL SKIRT

45" (115 cm) wide fabric

XXS to S

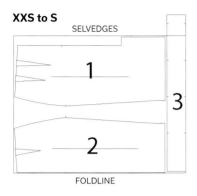

Fold fabric in half and cut pattern piece 2 on the fold. Cut pattern piece 1 as a pair and pattern piece 3 as a single piece. (Note: pattern piece 3 has been cut across the weft. Dependent on size, it can be cut going down the fabric next to pattern piece 1.)

M to 2XL

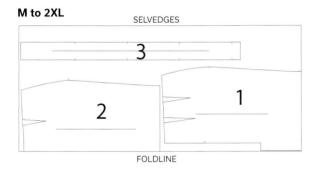

60" (150 cm) wide fabric

All Sizes

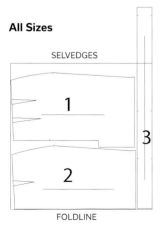

Fold fabric in half and cut pattern piece 2 on the fold. Cut pattern piece 1 as a pair and pattern piece 3 as a single piece.

THE FITTED TEE

60" (150 cm) wide fabric

XXS to S

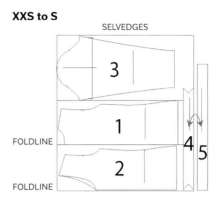

Fold fabric just enough to cut pattern piece 2 on the fold. Fold fabric just enough to cut pattern piece 1 on the fold. Fold remaining fabric in half and cut pattern piece 3. Cut either 4 or 5 pattern piece out of remaining end.

M to 2XL

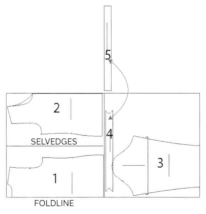

Fold fabric in half so selvedges meet in the center. Cut pattern piece 1 and 2 on the fold. Refold fabric in half. Cut pattern piece 3. Cut pattern piece 4 or 5 on remaining end.

THE CAMISOLE

45" (115 cm) wide fabric

XXS to S

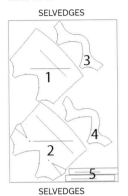

M to 2XL

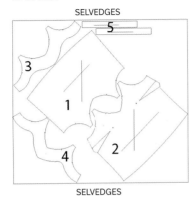

60" (150 cm) wide fabric

XXS to S

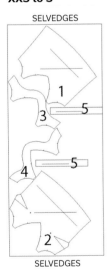

M to 2XL

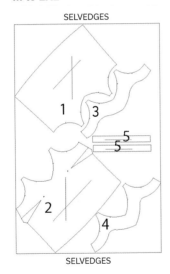

Open fabric to single lay and cut all pattern pieces.

THE WRAP DRESS

60" (150 cm) wide fabric

All Sizes

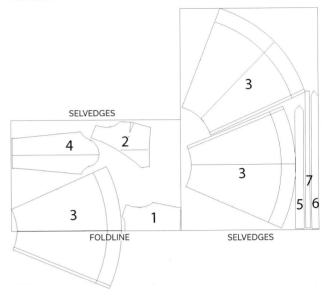

Fold fabric in half and cut pattern pieces 1, 2, 3, and 4. Open out fabric and cut single lay-mirror skirt pattern pieces no.3. Cut single pieces of 5, 6, and 7.

THE DUSTER

45" (115 cm) wide fabric

XXS to S

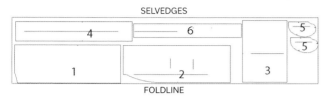

Fold fabric in half and cut all pattern pieces. Pattern piece 1 is cut on the fold.

M to 2XL

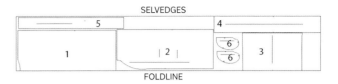

Fold fabric in half and cut all pattern pieces. Pattern piece 1 is cut on the fold. (Note: Due to the narrowness of the fabric, the sleeves have been turned to be cut with weft.)

60" (150 cm) wide fabric

XXS to S

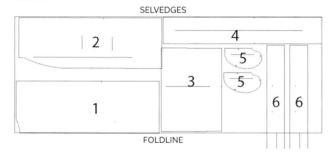

Fold fabric in half and cut all pattern pieces. Pattern piece 1 is cut on the fold. Pattern piece 6 is cut when remaining fabric is opened.

M to 2XL

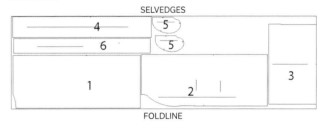

Fold fabric in half and cut all pattern pieces. Pattern piece 1 is cut on the fold.

resources

FABRIC SHOPS
Fabric Mart
fabricmart.com

I See Fabric
iseefabric.com

LA Finch Fabrics
lafinchfabrics.com

Melanated Fabrics
melanatedfabric.com

Oak Fabrics
oakfabrics.com

Sewing Studio
sewingstudio.com

Stone Mountain Fabric
stonemountainfabric.com

SEWING SUPPLIES & NOTIONS
Amazon
amazon.com

Leather & Sewing
Supply Depot
sewingsupplydepot.com

Melanated Fabrics
melanatedfabrics.com

Wawak
wawak.com

SEWING & PATTERN MAKING CLASSES
Pattern Making Academy
learnpatternmaking.com

Sew It Academy
sewitacademy.com

YOUTUBE CHANNELS YOU SHOULD KNOW!
Brittany J Jones
youtube.com/
brittanyjjoneslivelovesew

Lydia Naomi
youtube.com/lydianaomi

Mimi G
youtube.com/mimigstyleshow

Norris Danta Ford
youtube.com/norrisdantaford

Seamwork
youtube.com/seamworkvideo

INDIE & COMMERCIAL PATTERNS
Cashmerette
cashmerette.com

Deer and Doe
deer-and-doe.com

Friday Pattern Co.
fridaypatterncompany.com

Named Clothing
namedclothing.com

Papercut Patterns
papercutpatterns.com

Seamwork
seamwork.com

Simplicity
simplicity.com

Something Delightful
somethingdelightful.com

True Bias
truebias.com

VikiSews
vikisews.com

about the author

Mimi G. Ford is the creator of Mimi G Style, Inc. and award-winning business born from her love of sewing and design. Mimi is the founder of the fashion, lifestyle, and DIY website Mimi G. Style, the founder of Sew It! Academy, Vice President of Pattern, Design, and Brand Management for Design Group Americas and the host of the widely popular podcast Business S.H.E.T. She lives in Atlanta with her family.

acknowledgments

Words cannot express my gratitude to everyone who helped me along this journey. Special thanks to Tricia Camacho, pattern maker extraordinaire, for all your hard work. My husband, Norris Ford, for always being my biggest supporter, and my besties, Brittany and Faith, for keeping me on track and making me laugh along the way. Most importantly, I would like to thank all my fans and followers for your continued support; I would not be here without you.

Thanks!